Women Writers

VIRGINIA WOOLF

Clare Hanson

MACMILLAN

© Clare Hanson 1994

First published 1994 by
THE MACMILLAN PRESS LTD
Houndmills, Basingstoke, Hampshire RG21 2XS
and London
Companies and representatives
throughout the world

ISBN 0–333–45157–0 hardcover
ISBN 0–333–45158–9 paperback

A catalogue record for this book is available
from the British Library

Printed in Hong Kong

VIRGINIA WOOLF

Women Writers

General Editors: *Eva Figes and Adele King*

Published titles

Margaret Atwood, Barbara Hill Rigney
Jane Austen, Meenakshi Mukherjee
Elizabeth Bowen, Phyllis Lassner
Anne Brontë, Elizabeth Langland
Charlotte Brontë, Pauline Nestor
Emily Brontë, Lyn Pykett
Willa Cather, Susie Thomas
Colette, Diana Holmes
Ivy Compton-Burnett, Kathy Justice Gentile
Emily Dickinson, Joan Kirkby
George Eliot, Kristin Brady
Elizabeth Gaskell, Jane Spencer
Sylvia Plath, Susan Bassnett
Gertrude Stein, Jane Palatini Bowers
Eudora Welty, Louise Westling
Edith Wharton, Katherine Joslin
Women in Romanticism, Meena Alexander
Virginia Woolf, Clare Hanson

Forthcoming

Elizabeth Barrett Browning, Marjorie Stone
Nadine Gordimer, Kathy Wagner
Doris Lessing, Margaret Moan Rowe
Katherine Mansfield, Diane DeBell
Toni Morrison, Nellie McKay
Jean Rhys, Carol Rumens
Christina Rossetti, Linda Marshall
Stevie Smith, Romana Huk

Contents

Acknowledgements

I would like to thank the following for (variously) inspiration, advice and support during the writing of this book: Nicola Bradbury, Françoise Defromont, Sharon Ouditt, Joanne Shattock, Martin Stannard and Nicole Ward Jouve. I would also like to thank the many students whose enthusiasm and ideas have contributed to the shaping of this book.

Editors' Preface

The study of women's writing has been long neglected by a male critical establishment both in academic circles and beyond. As a result, many women writers have either been unfairly neglected or have been marginalised in some way, so that their true influence and importance has been ignored. Other women writers have been accepted by male critics and academics, but on terms which seem, to many women readers of this generation, to be false or simplistic. In the past the internal conflicts involved in being a woman in a male-dominated society have been largely ignored by readers of both sexes, and this has affected our reading of women's work. The time has come for a serious reassessment of women's writing in the light of what we understand today.

This series is designed to help in that reassessment.

All the books are written by women because we believe that men's understanding of feminist critique is only, at best, partial. And besides, men have held the floor quite long enough.

EVA FIGES
ADELE KING

Preface

Virginia Woolf haunts feminist criticism. There have been countless studies of her life and work, each seeking to define the 'real' Virginia Woolf; also, perhaps, to appropriate this person and her writing for their own purposes. So we have a range of current versions of the cultural phenomenon 'Virginia Woolf', from the engagé, socialist-feminist critic produced by Jane Marcus[1] to the writer of psychic theatre analysed by Daniel Ferrer in his recent study of the relations between Woolf's writing and madness.[2] Of course, this study is not exempt from the objection that it is driven and limited by a particular ideological perspective: to help the reader to identify this as rapidly as possible, I want here to outline briefly the argument of this book.

Much recent feminist criticism has positioned itself in relation to Lacan's influential reworking of Freudian psychoanalytic theory and in particular his account of the workings of the 'symbolic order' of language. Lacan's work suggests that 'women' are excluded *by* the symbolic order: by this he means that they are not represented within it, although this does not mean that they are excluded *from* it.[3] French feminist theorists such as Hélène Cixous and Luce Irigaray have responded to this by arguing that women must insert femininity-as-difference into the symbolic order, in order to destabilise and subvert that order. The writing of Virginia Woolf seems to offer a prelude to this endeavour: her texts inscribe femininity as un-fixed, problematic yet full of possibility. Her writing often seems to anticipate Cixous' experimental *écriture feminine*, or Irigaray's concern with a 'feminine morphology'.

My argument here is that in Woolf's early work this is indeed the case. In their exploration of the relationship between gender and representation and in their attempt to redefine the 'I' in writing, Woolf's texts overlap suggestively with those of Cixous, while she also maps out some of the territory later theorised by Irigaray in her exploration of relationships between women. I trace some of these connections in the first half of this book. However, I also suggest that in writing *To the Lighthouse* – a pivotal book – Woolf became increasingly conscious of the difficulties attendant on an exploration/celebration of femininity as difference. In her later work she is thus more wary about 'the feminine' as a category, recognising, I think, the dangers of (re)creating a category which is exclusive, restrictive and divisive, as limiting as any masculine construction of 'femininity'.

In Woolf's later work there is, then, a shift in emphasis, which might be defined as a movement away from an interest in *the difference of femininity*, towards an interest in *femininity as difference* in a wider, philosophical sense. Woolf's later texts invent shifting patterns which seem to enact the idea of meaning itself as difference, against the monism of what we would now call the phallogocentric symbolic order.

I wish to emphasise the complexity of Woolf's exploration of the key issues of subjectivity and sexual difference, which she saw as constitutive of meaning itself. The sketch offered above, moving from a Cixousian to a more broadly deconstructive, or postmodern view of difference, clearly offers only one way into Woolf's extraordinarily rich and sustained meditation on the issues which still drive feminist theory and criticism. Woolf's work could not, in fact, be more centrally focused on the question which Margaret Whitford, in a recent review of feminist philosophy, sees as the 'structuring dichotomy' of modern thought about sexuality:

the dichotomy between essentialism and construc-
tionism (read: between Enlightenment and postmodernist paradigms, or between identity and its
dissemination).[4]

It is this dichotomy which also structures this book.

been able to do. Judith Woolf, who provided in both instances
a more careful review of the questions raised by Naomi
Schor's and others' here, received review of feminist
philosophy, as a tool for generating debates of
modern thought about sexuality.

the distinctiveness of women's culture and to say
it, and even a very profound distinction with philosophy
feminist persuasion, as I have often heard women say
their claims.

D. J. ENRIGHT and DOUGLAS RAWLINSON

1 Introduction

A Sketch of the Life

Virginia Woolf's life and work cannot easily be disentangled. It is difficult in her case to practise the kind of critical hygiene urged by the New Critics, and to treat her work as a free-standing, autonomous entity – most obviously because the widespread knowledge of her 'madness' and of her suicide casts an inescapable shadow over her writing. Aspects of Woolf's well-documented life[1] have by now attained the status of intertexts, which interweave with her fiction and influence our interpretation of it. There is a kind of precedent for this interweaving of life and art in Woolf's own blurring of the boundaries between them: in her production of diaries, letters and memoirs Woolf created a kind of interface between life and text, and herself questioned the barriers between them. She was aware that her writing was intensely retrospective and rooted in personal experience, and in 1920 asked herself whether in her writing she simply dealt in autobiography, and called it fiction.[2]

This dissolving of the boundaries between life and art is characteristic of women writers, who have excelled in the art forms of diaries, letters and journals, centred around 'everyday', domestic experience. However, in the case of Woolf, and her contemporaries Mansfield and H.D., something more seems to be at stake in this pursuit of the personal. The example of psychoanalysis is crucial here, particularly Freud's case histories (of women patients).

Psychoanalysis offered two things for female modernist
writers: a new subject area, or rather, new ways of
defining/interpreting female subjectivity, and new
techniques such as free association, the use of dreams
and symptomatic writing. Analysis offered, I would
suggest, the framework out of which a new female
Bildungsroman could be built, loosely composed of
intersecting elements of fictional/poetic, journal and
meditative writing. Such a *Bildungsroman* might be
composed precisely *not* as a single, unified text, but out
of different texts, interlocking in a mosaic-like
structure.

Woolf herself might not have recognised this
structure – it may be one which is created only with
hindsight. However, the notion that the female
modernist *Bildungsroman* might be an extensive and
transgressive *oeuvre*, composed of different kinds of
writing, has informed the discussion of Woolf's life in
this chapter. The focus is therefore both on those
aspects of her life which have fed most clearly and
directly into her fiction and on those which have lent
themselves to autobiographical or other kinds of
textual elaboration. First, then, following a traditional
analytic principle, her family, and in particular, her
mother.

In the Cage: Early Family Life

> *Now I shall try to describe the cage – 22 Hyde Park Gate*
> ('A Sketch of the Past')

Virginia Woolf was born in January 1882, the third
child and second daughter of Leslie and Julia Stephen.
Since both her parents had been married before, and
widowed, she grew up in a large family which
included not only her older sister and brother,

Vanessa and Thoby, and her younger brother Adrian, but also Leslie Stephen's daughter Laura (thought to be 'retarded'), and Julia Stephen's children George, Stella and Gerald Duckworth. She was born into a late-Victorian, upper-middle-class family, in which there were, according to Quentin Bell, two competing traditions, one of talent, and one of beauty.[3] Through her father, Woolf was linked with literary talent: Leslie Stephen was an essayist and 'man of letters' whose first wife had been a daughter of Thackeray. His friends included James and Meredith, but probably more important for Woolf than early memories of tea with Henry James was her father's example of a disciplined and professional commitment to writing.

Woolf's attitude to her father was, as she herself said, ambivalent. At times he seemed the model of a Victorian patriarch, selfish, demanding, endlessly claiming sympathy and support from his wife and daughters. In the years after Julia Stephen's death in 1895 he drew mercilessly on his daughters for sympathy in his widowed state, and seemed to Woolf:

the tyrant father – the exacting, the violent, the histrionic, the demonstrative, the self-centred, the self-pitying, the deaf.[4]

Yet she often felt affection for her father, for his 'character', which she outlined in the following way in 'A Sketch of the Past':

I too felt his attractiveness. It arose – to name some elements at random – from his simplicity, his integrity, his eccentricity – by which I mean he would say exactly what he thought, however inconvenient; and do what he liked. (*MB*, p. 123)

Although she was 'obsessed' with her father as well as her mother – her parents seem to have impressed themselves on her as archetypal, polarised Victorian Man and Woman – Leslie Stephen does not, on the whole, seem to have haunted Woolf as her mother did. There is one extraordinary diary entry in which Woolf contemplates calmly what her fate would have been if her father had not died in 1904:

> Father's birthday. He would have been 96, 96, yes, today; and could have been 96, like other people one has known: but mercifully was not. His life would have entirely ended mine. What would have happened? No writing; no books; – inconceivable.[5]

Yet the sense here is not of personal antagonism, but of a complete understanding of the operation of a social system. Under patriarchy at that time, it would have been impossible for Woolf to pursue any kind of career had her father lived and needed her care: the diary entry shows not hatred, but simple recognition of that fact. Woolf's feelings for her father seem on the whole more equable, less intense, than those for her mother: he is always presented from a distance, and characterised with an objectivity which Woolf could not achieve in discussion of her mother.

Virgina Woolf's mother represented 'beauty', but beauty associated, according to Quentin Bell, with 'a certain moral grandeur'. In Bell's biography, in Woolf's memoirs, and as she is presented in fictional terms in *To the Lighthouse*, Woolf's mother is at the centre of the family, and that centrality is bound up with her beauty and with her physical presence. Woolf 'remembers' her thus in 'A Sketch of the Past':

> Certainly there she was, in the very centre of that great Cathedral space which was childhood; there

she was from the very first. My first memory is of her lap; the scratch of some beads on her dress comes back to me as I pressed my cheek against it . . .

. . . how did I first become conscious of what was always there – her astonishing beauty? Perhaps I never became conscious of it; I think I accepted her beauty as the natural quality that a mother – she seemed typical, universal, yet our own in particular – had by virtue of being our mother. It was part of her calling. I do not think that I separated her face from that general being; or from her whole body. (*MB*, p. 91)

I shall come back to the influence of the mother later in this chapter, but it is worth noting here that Woolf is unable to distinguish between the physical body of her mother and her maternal role: it is as though the mother's body and beauty literally give shape and meaning to existence. It is also notable, however, that Woolf uses terms here which recur in her celebrated depiction of the 'Angel in the House', who shares her mother's grace and sanctity, but must of course be violently destroyed:

Above all – I need not say it – she was pure. Her purity was supposed to be her chief beauty – her blushes, her great grace. In those days – the last of Queen Victoria – every house had its angel. And when I came to write I encountered her with the very first words. The shadow of her wings fell on my page; I heard the rustling of her skirts in the room . . .

. . . I turned upon her and caught her by the throat. I did my best to kill her. My excuse, if I were to be had up in a court of law, would be that I acted in

self-defence. Had I not killed her she would have
killed me. She would have plucked the heart out of
my writing.[6]

The violence of the metaphor reveals the strength of
Woolf's feeling that certain aspects of her mother's
'beauty' were inimical to female self-expression, and
must be rooted out of her own developing personality.

More often in her memoirs, however, Woolf
describes her mother in terms which place her as/at
the origin of life: in one striking passage of her
'Reminiscences' (written for her nephew Julian Bell),
her mother takes the place of Christ, as Woolf
recreates the scene of her death and places it in a post-
crucifixion landscape:

> If what I have said of her has any meaning you will
> believe that her death was the greatest disaster that
> could happen; it was as though on some brilliant
> day of spring the racing clouds of a sudden stood
> still, grew dark, and massed themselves; the wind
> flagged, and all creatures on the earth moaned or
> wandered seeking aimlessly. (*MB*, p. 47)

Her mother was at one and the same time 'central'
and absent. In 'A Sketch of the Past' Woolf describes
her sense of living so 'completely in her atmosphere
that one never got far enough away from her to see her
as a person': at the same time, Woolf felt that she
could never get close enough to her on a personal
level:

> she was living on such an extended surface that she
> had not time, nor strength, to concentrate, except
> for a moment if one were ill or in some child's crisis,
> upon me. (*MB*, p. 92)

Louise DeSalvo has argued that, by modern standards, Julia Stephen's 'nurturing' of her large family was inadequate: she believed strongly in discipline, and provided, in DeSalvo's words, only 'chilly and distant supervision' for her children. While this is to take her behaviour out of context, and thus, I think, to misrepresent it, certainly Woolf could never get enough affection from her mother, which may itself account for her heavy investment in the maternal principle *in fantasy*. Julia Stephen's remoteness may well have been the seed for the sense of loss which became uncontainable when she died. After her death, Woolf described herself again as 'haunted' by her, remembering her, according to her own account, almost daily:

> on more occasions than I can number, in bed at night, or in the street, or as I come into the room, there she is; beautiful, emphatic, with her familiar phrase and her laugh; closer than any of the living are . . . (*MB*, p. 47)

Loss: 'this baffling, frustrating whirlpool'

> *Very soon after Stella's death we realised that we must make some standing place for ourselves in this baffling, frustrating whirlpool* ('A Sketch of the Past')

Further consideration of Woolf's family life reinforces our sense of the centrality of loss in her early experience. When her mother died in 1895 it seemed that life itself had failed, according to Woolf, but the death of her half-sister, Stella, in 1897 had a yet deeper and more damaging effect. After Julia Stephen's death, Leslie Stephen directed his imperious demands for comfort initially at Stella, who had been her mother's confidante, and who resembled her in a number of ways. Woolf describes the confused situation in 'Reminiscences' – her father given over to grief to the extent that the Stephen children had virtually lost both parents; Stella given over to *his* comfort and support:

> I do not think that Stella lost consciousness for a single moment during all those months of his immediate need. (*MB*, p. 48)

Woolf's account in 'Reminiscences' has an oblique sub-text: she hints that Stella came to replace her mother in a quasi-sexual way for Leslie Stephen as she was 'placed in the utmost intimacy' with a man whom 'she had hitherto regarded only with respect and a formal affection.' Indeed, the hidden agenda of 'Reminiscences' could be said to be an exploration, or discovery, of the ways in which Julia Stephen, Stella Duckworth and Vanessa Stephen came in turn to occupy the same place for both Woolf *and* her father. These women were at once maternal and erotic figures for father and daughter, offering, or seeming to offer, an ultimate nurturing which would incorporate nothing less than *jouissance*.[7] The mother/wife figure is constructed in Woolf's memory as a site of ecstasy, an endlessly receptive and giving body – but the mother's subjectivity, *her* needs for attention or nurture, are not registered. In her study of Woolf and child abuse, Louise DeSalvo suggests a link between such neglect of the needs of adult women within patriarchy, and self-perpetuating cycles of abuse and lack of care for female children.[8]

For a time Stella Duckworth was utterly subordinated to Stephen and his needs, but then she became engaged and, to Leslie Stephen's annoyance, married.

She went abroad, became pregnant, then fell ill: according to Woolf this illness was 'mismanaged', and Stella died in July 1897. Woolf describes the effect in detail in 'A Sketch of the Past':

> My mother's death had been a latent sorrow – at thirteen one could not master it, envisage it, deal with it. But Stella's death two years later fell on a different substance; a mind stuff and being stuff that was extraordinarily unprotected, unformed, unshielded, apprehensive, receptive, anticipatory ... But beneath the surface of this particular mind and body lay sunk the other death ... All this had toned my mind and made it apprehensive; made it I suppose unnaturally responsive to Stella's happiness, and the promise it held for her and for us of escape from that gloom; when once more unbelievably – incredibly – as if one had been violently cheated of some promise ... the blow, the second blow of death, struck on me. (*MB*, p. 137)

Two strands of imagery recur in Woolf's accounts of loss: that of water/drowning, and that of being cheated, having something snatched away. DeSalvo has convincingly shown that the metaphors of drowning, and of the whirlpool, were connected for Woolf with the abuse which she suffered from her half-brothers, but these watery metaphors also take us straight back to the mother (who could of course be blamed for having 'permitted' the early abuse, or for not preventing it). In some respects, water seems to represent the safe, sealed medium or space of the mother, even perhaps the watery state before birth, so that Woolf's obsessional use of the image might be related to what Hélène Cixous has called 'the eternal, impossible mourning of when someone else was I – an articulation between child and mother'.[9] In other words, one might see Woolf's recurrent use of the metaphors of water and waves as expressing, subliminally, the desire to return to a state when the I can also be the other and the articulation of subjectivity is not fatally compromised by the ego. Such an interpretation would accommodate a reading of the 'cheating', 'snatching' metaphors as in some way connected also with maternal deprivation.

'Something about the body': Woolf and Sexuality

> *To speak without figure she had thought of something, something about the body, about the passions which it was unfitting for her as a woman to say.* ('Professions for Women')

Woolf was preoccupied with the question of 'writing the [female] body', but the difficulty was, from the beginning, how that body was to be constructed or construed. Woolf's experience of child abuse certainly compromised and threatened a conventional sense of female sexual identity, and DeSalvo argues that her 'choice' of a celibate life was in direct response to the sexual attentions of her half-brothers.[10] From the evidence provided by DeSalvo, and also of course by Quentin Bell, it is clear that Woolf was abused by Gerald Duckworth when she was only six, and that in adolescence she was subjected to repeated abuse by George Duckworth. Quentin Bell describes the abuse by George:

> There were fondlings and fumblings in public when Virginia was at her lessons and these were carried to greater lengths – indeed I know not to what lengths – when, with the easy assurance of a fond

and privileged brother, George carried his affections from the schoolroom into the night nursery.[11]

DeSalvo is rather hard on Quentin Bell, claiming that in presenting the information about incest he 'blamed the victim Woolf for her response' rather than condemning her half-brothers. Yet it should be noted that well before the publication of Alice Miller's pioneering work on child abuse, Bell saw the possible connection between Woolf's 'madness' and her abuse, and commented feelingly on Woolf's 'appalling' situation.

DeSalvo's study is indispensable for an understanding of the extent of the abuse Woolf suffered, and of its possible long-term effects. However, there are some blind spots, especially in matters of interpretation. As indicated above, DeSalvo claims that Woolf's celibate life-style was 'chosen' as a result of the abuse she suffered; elsewhere, she suggests that Woolf:

> *chose* lesbian love, with Violet Dickinson and with Vita Sackville-West, as a positive, *adaptive* response to her abuse.[12]

Apart from the rather dubious notion of 'choice' in such a context, the implication here is that lesbianism cannot be normal, even though it is described as positive: it is still something which comes about as the result of a fault or aberration.

However, it is extremely difficult to interpret or discuss the facts of Woolf's adult sexuality: little can be said with any confidence because there is such scanty evidence to go on. We have very little knowledge either of her life with Leonard Woolf or of her later relationships with women. Moreover, Woolf did not explore her own sexuality in her

autobiography, something which she felt was a limita-
tion, writing to Ethel Smyth in 1941:

> But as so much of life is sexual – or so they say – it
> rather limits autobiography if this is blacked out.[13]

Sue Roe, in a complex study, has argued that Woolf's
creative writing was damaged by her inability to
confront or explore her sexuality. At the heart of
Woolf's writing, she suggests, there lies an empty
space:

> Empty, that is, of the kinds of narrative which
> would have explained or given Virginia Woolf
> access to the source of her own dilemma ... but
> crowded with kaleidoscopic images which seem to
> offer visions which, when observed very closely, are
> seen to function only as distractions.[14]

It could be argued, however, that Woolf does 'write
the body' in and through her fiction, continually
suggesting new, shadowy 'somethings' about the
body, about female experience. Given the crucial role
which fantasy plays in our relation to sexuality and
the body, it would be mistaken, I think, to read
Woolf's texts as 'spinster' texts, as some earlier critics
have done. Perhaps, too, there is something in the
originality of Woolf's writing about 'the passions' – its
woman-centredness, or its attempt to evoke a 'feminine
economy' – which has made for some misinterpreta-
tion.

   Woolf does, of course, write about sexuality in a
coded way, as did other female modernist writers such
as Mansfield or Djuna Barnes. An obvious example
would be the description of Sally Seton's kiss in *Mrs
Dalloway*:

Then came the most exquisite moment of her whole life passing a stone urn with flowers in it. Sally stopped; picked a flower; kissed her on the lips. The whole world might have turned upside down! The others disappeared; there she was alone with Sally. And she felt that she had been given a present, wrapped up, and told just to keep it, not to look at it – a diamond, something infinitely precious, wrapped up, which, as they walked (up and down, up and down), she uncovered, or the radiance burnt through, the revelation, the religious feeling! – when old Joseph and Peter faced them.[15]

This has been read by Catherine Stimpson as a coded description of lesbian love.[16] It is a moment of feeling for another woman released through a physical gesture which 'turns the whole world upside down': the text both enacts and images (through syntactical elaborations and the wrapping metaphor) the veiling process on which the moment depends for its erotic charge.

The 'exquisite' moment is connected with veiling and not looking: it exists without reference to male demand or the male gaze. Another such moment occurs in *To the Lighthouse* when Woolf evokes very strongly – again using the suggestive power of imagery and elaborate syntax – the female experience of orgasm. Mrs Ramsay is alone: the ecstatic experience is created as she looks at the lighthouse beam, especially as she gazes at the third stroke, which is 'so much her, yet so little her'. Mary Jacobus has suggested that this is an 'autoerotic' moment:[17] certainly it exists without reference to any male object:

For all that, she thought, watching it with fascination, hypnotised, as if it were stroking with its silver

> fingers some sealed vessel in her brain whose
> bursting would flood her with delight, she had
> known happiness, exquisite happiness, intense
> happiness, and it silvered the rough waves a little
> more brightly, as daylight faded, and the blue went
> out of the sea and it rolled in waves of pure lemon
> which curved and swelled and broke upon the
> beach and the ecstasy burst in her eyes and waves
> of pure delight raced over the floor of her mind and
> she felt, It is enough! It is enough!
>
> He turned and saw her . . .[18]

Again the male gaze interrupts or checks a moment of ecstasy.

I want to suggest that we can interpret Woolf's writing here in relation to the Cixousian notion of 'writing the body', and also in relation to the idea of an *écriture féminine*. I am not arguing here that Woolf's writing can be read as an 'example' proving the correctness of recent French feminist theory. However, I would suggest that Woolf's texts engage with the same problem as that articulated by Cixous, Irigaray and Kristeva, namely, how is the feminine to be written in our culture? Lacanian psychoanalytic theory, as we have seen, suggests either that 'woman' does not exist, or that 'she' is not represented/representable within the existing symbolic order. Cixous and other contemporary feminists have countered this by attempting to affirm women's *positive* difference from men, and by attempting to articulate a specifically *feminine* subjectivity. Woolf in her early work seems to be similarly concerned to insert feminine difference into a culture which is psychologically *indifferent*, in Irigaray's phrase, i.e. which does not recognise (sexual) difference. One of Woolf's means of doing this is to focus on the maternal body/

the female body, the materiality of which is normally repressed within the phallogocentric symbolic order. The invocation of the material/maternal female body in the passages quoted above puts pressure on the limits of the symbolic order.

Woolf's writing seems particularly close to the creative and critical work of Hélène Cixous, especially in its use of fluid figurative language to evoke 'the feminine' as a potential not yet released in/through language. Cixous has of course suggested that women inhabit a libidinal economy which is peculiarly open to difference and admission of the other. Such an economy she calls 'the other bisexuality', one which does not seek to annul difference, but which accepts and celebrates it:

> Bisexuality – that is to say, the location within oneself of the presence of both sexes, evident and insistent in different ways according to the individual, the nonexclusion of difference or of a sex.[19]

It has to be stressed that it is not biology, but the cultural construction of sexual and reproductive roles which produces an 'economy without reserve' like that described by Cixous. Such an 'economy' is also implicit in the experience of Woolf's female characters. It is striking that Woolf and Cixous use the same terms to suggest such an (ideal) mode of being: images of the gift and of the waves preponderate. Cixous' use of the waves to figure a 'feminine' libidinal economy overlaps suggestively with Woolf's repeated use of the metaphor. Cixous writes, for example:

> There is a bond between woman's libidinal economy – her *jouissance*, the feminine Imaginary – and her way of self-constituting a subjectivity that splits

apart without regret, and without this regretless-
ness being the equivalent of dying . . .

Unleashed and raging, she belongs to the race of
waves. She arises, she approaches, she lifts up, she
reaches, covers over, washes a shore, flows
embracing the cliff's least undulation, already she is
another, arising again, throwing the fringed vastness of her body up high, follows herself, and covers
over, uncovers, polishes, makes the stone body
shine with the gentle undeserting ebbs . . .[20]

The image of the waves suggests precisely the 'splitting
apart without regret' associated both with the
'feminine' personality and with female sexuality in the
work of Woolf.

Cixous also links the 'feminine' economy with
writing. She claims that:

There is a link between the economy of femininity
– the open, extravagant subjectivity, that relationship to the other in which the gift doesn't calculate
its influence – and the possibility of love; and a link
today between this 'libido of the other' and
writing.[21]

This again is particularly suggestive in relation to
Woolf, for whom the phrase 'writing the body' can
have at least two senses. Woolf not only writes (about)
the body but has a lover-like relation to the body of
language, a 'respect' for *its* bodily origins.

'Reduced to whirlpool': 'Madness' and Suicide

*Freud is upsetting: reducing one to whirlpool; & I daresay
truly. If we're all instinct, the unconscious, whats all this
about civilisation, the whole man, freedom. (Diary)*

Madness, as Michel Foucault has demonstrated, is a relative category. In *Madness and Civilisation* he argues that one of the ways in which the modern state maintains itself is through the categorisation of deviant individuals who threaten its stability. These individuals are assigned to categories and institutions (madman–asylum, criminal–prison) which will contain them and defuse their obstructive potential. It can be argued that the (stereo)typing of Virginia Woolf as 'mad' was part of a similar manoeuvre, whereby Woolf's subversive responses to some of the pressures put on her by patriarchy and, particularly, by her male relations, could be contained and effectively discounted. This view of Woolf's illness as produced by the pressures of patriarchy has been promoted particularly by American feminist critics. Elaine Showalter, in *A Literature of Their Own* (1977) was the first to point out that nearly all our information about Woolf's madness comes from two male figures: her husband and her nephew. Both, unequivocally, state that Woolf was 'mad', but they fail to notice that, as Showalter writes,

> Her major breakdowns were associated with crises in female identity: the first occurred in 1895, after the death of her mother and the onset of menstruation; the second from 1913–1915, after Leonard decided that they should not have children. Her suicide in 1940 followed menopause; though less information about it has been published, it seems to have repeated elements of the earlier episodes.[22]

Showalter argues that Leonard Woolf, in particular, was 'complicit' with Woolf's sickness. Failing to accept the fact that her distress between 1913 and 1915 was bound up with the sexual failure of their marriage and *his* decision not to have children, Leonard Woolf effectively shifted the blame for her distress on to Woolf herself, diagnosing her dis-ease as madness and searching out as treatment a prohibitive 'rest-cure' like that which nearly kills the protagonist in Charlotte Perkins Gilman's story *The Yellow Wallpaper* (1891).

Showalter argues, then, that the notion of Woolf's madness has acted as a convenient screen, covering up some of the disturbances which happened when Woolf's sense of female identity was threatened or compromised by those closest to her. In his detailed study *All That Summer She Was Mad* (1981), Stephen Trombley supports Showalter's contentions, emphasising the way in which the male medical profession colluded with Leonard Woolf in his attempts to police his wife:

> In many cases, the diagnosis of insanity represents nothing more than an attempt on the part of the medical profession *to enforce unwritten social codes* as if they were the law of the land.[23]

Trombley's book offers particularly useful information about the doctors who treated Woolf, and places it in the context both of current and contemporary discourses about madness.

Recently, Louise DeSalvo has extended the debate about the causes of Woolf's madness. She writes that:

> Any view which explains Virginia Woolf's behaviour as madness is archaic: too much is now known about the behaviour of victims of childhood abuse to support such a description.[24]

DeSalvo links Woolf's suicide attempts with her incestuous experiences. She cites Woolf's description of the violent feelings of rage and hatred caused by George Duckworth's abuse, and her statement that the breakdown which followed her mother's death was 'not unnaturally the result of all these emotions and complications'. She also connects Woolf's suicidal feelings in 1936 with the fact that she had then seen Gerald Duckworth for the first time in twenty years: meeting him was, Woolf wrote, like 'visiting an alligator in a tank, an obese and obsolete alligator'. Although Woolf had not yet brought the memory of Gerald's early abuse to consciousness, her encounter with him brought about feelings of powerlessness and exposure which, DeSalvo argues, became over-powering when the memory finally reached consciousness in 1941.

DeSalvo suggests that in the diary entry quoted at the beginning of this section, Woolf finds reading Freud so threatening because of his recantation of the 'seduction theory' and substitution for it of the 'drive theory'. Freud's rejection of his patients' stories of seduction in infancy, and suggestion that these stories were fantasies, could well have undermined Woolf's sense of her own sanity. DeSalvo suggests that at this point in her life:

> [Woolf] was ascribing her depression and her 'madness' to her abuse. [Freud] was describing reports of incest as fantasies which were wish-fulfillment. She wondered whose view was correct and there is evidence that, after a lifetime of struggle ... she wavered, reconsidered, and accepted Freud. This meant that she would have to see herself as mad.[25]

If the American feminist response to Woolf's 'mad-ness' has been to relate it to social and cultural

pressures, French feminists have characteristically
read it in terms of psychic processes essentially
detached from social pressures. Julia Kristeva's
comments on Woolf's life and writing in the essay
'About Chinese Women' have proved particularly
influential. Kristeva writes:

> Once the moorings of the word, the ego, the
> superego, begin to slip, life itself can't hang on:
> death quietly moves in. Suicide without a cause, or
> sacrifice without fuss for an apparent cause which,
> in our age, is usually political: a woman can carry
> off such things without tragedy, even without
> drama, without the feeling that she is fleeing a well-
> fortified front, but rather as though it were simply a
> matter of making an inevitable, irresistible and self-
> evident transition.
>
> I think of Virginia Woolf, who sank wordlessly
> into the river, her pockets weighed down with
> stones. Haunted by voices, waves, lights, in love
> with colours – blue, green – and seized by a strange
> gaiety that would bring on the fits of strangled,
> screeching laughter recalled by Miss Brown.[26]

Kristeva's argument is that women writers are in a
particularly privileged, and also dangerous position,
for they are more likely than male writers to remain in
touch with the 'semiotic', with early, pre-Oedipal
experience and its proto-organisation. Their texts are
thus articulated across the interplay between the
semiotic and symbolic: this brings a potential richness
and fullness to their work, but also threatens its
stability, because the semiotic always threatens the
subject with dissolution.

For Kristeva, the pre-Oedipal semiotic realm
clearly carries a negative charge. It threatens dis-

integration and loss and has a very different inflection from Cixous' positively viewed 'articulation with the mother' (see p. 101 above). The problem with Kristeva's view – and with those commentators who have followed her – is that in her linking of the feminine and the semiotic a kind of 'downgrading' seems to take place whereby the feminine becomes connected in disappointingly recognisable ways with nonsense, madness and death. For a woman, *writing* becomes an almost pathological activity, a masochistic flirting with death.

Kristeva's view of Woolf's 'madness' is disturbing because of the sense she gives that there is something irresistible, inescapable and connected in the semiotic chain women–writer–madness–death. As we have seen, American feminist commentary on Woolf is similarly pessimistic and deterministic in its interpretation of her 'madness', though the determining causes there are seen as social rather than psychic. It is almost as though in its concern for Woolf, feminist criticism has done her a disservice in inextricably connecting her madness and her gender. In considering her writing, is it not more appropriate to ask the kind of questions posed by Daniel Ferrer, which assume an intimate connection between *all* writing and madness, not least because writing must, by its status as discourse, exclude madness absolutely and continually? Ferrer goes on to link Woolf's madness – but not her gender – and the *form* of her writing:

> the relation to madness, in various forms, including the threat to the very existence of the author, is an essential element of this *oeuvre*, inseparable from the upsets and shock-waves it causes to the forms of narrative fiction.[27]

Such an approach offers a way out of what seems to have become a 'reductive whirlpool' of feminist consideration of Woolf's madness.

Woolf and the Scene of Writing

One of the most helpful ways of approaching Woolf's writing is through a consideration of the passages in 'A Sketch of the Past' where she describes her earliest memories. The link between memory and writing is always strong for Woolf, but, paradoxically, her emphasis on memory leads both here and in her novels to a suspension of chronological time in favour of a foregrounding of the depth and space of memory/writing. This is evident, I think, in the oscillations and waverings over tense in the opening paragraphs of 'A Sketch of the Past':

> So without stopping to choose my way, in the sure and certain knowledge that it will find itself – or if not it will not matter – *I begin*: the first memory.
>
> This *was* of red and purple flowers on a black ground – my mother's dress; and she *was sitting* either in a train or in an omnibus, and I *was* on her lap. I therefore *saw* the flowers she was wearing very close; and *can still see* purple and red and blue, *I think*, against the black; they *must have been* anemones, *I suppose*. Perhaps *we were going* to St Ives; more probably, for from the light it *must have been* evening, we *were coming* back to London. (*MB*, p. 72)

Chronology is more brutally subverted as Woolf goes on to insist that a second memory is *also* her first memory, that it exists in exactly the same space/time:

For that will lead to my other memory, which also seems to be my first memory, and in fact it is the most important of all my memories. If life has a base that it stands upon, if it is a bowl that one fills and fills and fills – then my bowl without a doubt stands upon this memory. It is of lying half asleep, half awake, in bed in the nursery at St Ives. It is of hearing the waves breaking, one, two, one, two, and sending a splash of water over the beach; and then breaking, one, two, one, two, behind a yellow blind. It is of hearing the blind draw its little acorn across the floor as the wind blew the blind out. It is of lying and hearing this splash and seeing this light, and feeling, it is almost impossible that I should be here; of feeling the purest ecstasy I can conceive. (*MB*, pp. 72–3)

Retrospectively, we can see that Woolf is offering us here a primal writing scene, an image or origin the details of which recur at central points throughout her fiction. For example, the waves and the rooks (Woolf goes on to describe the rooks in 'A Sketch') are there too, tinged – or fringed – with the same joy at the opening of *Mrs Dalloway*, as Clarissa *remembers* summer mornings at Bourton. Parallel scenes exist of course in *To the Lighthouse* and *The Waves*. More interestingly still, the scene has certain correspondences with Woolf's famous description of the act or moment of writing, in *A Room of One's Own*. There she writes:

Some collaboration has to take place in the mind between the woman and the man before the art of creation can be accomplished. Some marriage of opposites has to be consummated. The whole of the mind must lie wide open if we are to get the sense that the writer is communicating his experience

with perfect fullness. There must be freedom and
there must be peace. Not a wheel must grate, not a
light glimmer. The curtains must be close drawn.[28]

It is illuminating to juxtapose these scenes, which
share certain characteristics. In both the writer is
passive, lying back in a womb-like state which is also a
borderline state, on the border between waking and
sleeping, light and dark. These features open up
particular interpretive possibilities. It seems as though
Woolf places the ground of being and the origin of
writing in the same place/space, which is explicitly
related to the mother's body in 'A Sketch of the Past',
implicitly related to the sexual relation between her
parents in *A Room of One's Own*. One could, to be
literal, read the first scene as taking place next to her
parents' room at St Ives, as Woolf indicates; the
second scene (the *Room* scene) as related to the same
room in Hyde Park Gate, where Woolf spent much of
her childhood (see the reference to wheels, etc.). In the
first scene (the 'most important' one), ecstasy is
crucially dependent on the proximity of the mother.
Of course this is an imaginary mother – but the
centrality of the mother when Woolf thinks about the
origins of writing is striking. It is as though she has
already carried out the revolutionary *coup* called for by
the French feminist Antoinette Fouque – the re-
appropriation of the feminine symbolic via a renewal
of the writer's relation to the mother. Fouque, writing
in the shadow cast by Lacan, has called for:

A woman-identified mode of representation and
expression of the bond to the mother as a positive
identification. This originary love-story with
another woman, the mother, is at the heart of the
project of a symbolic revolution that would shift the

position of structural exclusion to which the feminine is confined.[29]

After a period in which, it could be argued, phallocentric structures have dominated western thought, many women, as I have suggested, have begun to feel the need for re-vision, and for reparation. One important task, discussed briefly above, has been to heal the apparent split between the mother and language, to link language back to maternal as well as paternal creativity. As Fouque argues:

> Why should it be the father who has the function of language? Who says so? The mother speaks to her child. The division of humanity between body and discourse is aberrant . . .[30]

The second, perhaps more difficult task, is to make visible the bond between mother and daughter which is the primary model for woman-centred relationships which might elude the appropriative structures of patriarchy. Fouque, like Cixous, argues for a woman-centred economy of relations centred on 'the other bisexuality' or a 'female homosexual libidinal economy'. Such relationships between women are not to be confused with lesbian relationships, which Fouque sees as potentially reactionary, to the extent that they mimic conventional phallocentric relations between the sexes. The woman-to-woman relations called for by Fouque and Cixous are founded on and are the necessary result of a positive identification to the maternal. Such 'homosexuality' is based on woman-identified values and ways of knowing and, paradoxically, the rehabilitation of this homosexuality/female libidinal economy is seen as the prelude to a new definition of heterosexuality, one that would recognise the importance of the differences between the sexes. Fouque, again:

> Woman's primary, fundamental homosexuality should only be a passage toward a rediscovered and truly free heterosexuality.[31]

While it has long been recognised that relations between women are important in the fiction of Woolf, such analyses as these can lead to fuller appreciation of the complex patternings and positionings which are made available in her texts. In *Mrs Dalloway*, for example, the relationships between Mrs Dalloway and Sally Seton, on the one hand, and between Elizabeth Dalloway and Miss Kilman, on the other, seem to act out the two possibilities discussed above, the relation between Mrs Dalloway and Sally Seton embodying a 'female homosexual economy' which is viewed positively and celebrated by the text, while that between Elizabeth and Miss Kilman is the model of a 'reactionary' lesbian relation which merely replicates the patterns of dominance of patriarchy:

> The cruellest things in the world, she thought, seeing them clumsy, hot, domineering, hypocritical, eavesdropping, jealous, infinitely cruel and unscrupulous, dressed in a mackintosh coat . . .[32]

Coming full circle, we come closer to the origins of Woolf's writing in the pivotal relation between Mrs Ramsay and Lily Briscoe in *To the Lighthouse*. In exploring this relation, Woolf recovers the connexions between the imaginary mother and writing (figured here as 'sacred inscription') and celebrates an 'intimacy' and inter-relatedness unknown in relations with men:

She imagined how in the chambers of the mind and heart of the woman who was, physically, touching her, were stood, like the treasures in the tombs of kings, tablets bearing sacred inscriptions, which if one could spell them out would teach one everything, but they would never be offered openly, never made public. What art was there, known to love or cunning, by which one pressed through into those secret chambers? What device for becoming, like waters poured into one jar, inextricably the same, one with the object one adored?[33]

It is from and to this scene of writing, the maternal space (or 'secret chambers') known to love, that Woolf's writing, initially, makes its way.

2 Moving Out: Rachel and Jacob

In *The Voyage Out* and in *Jacob's Room* Woolf provides early studies of sexual types and of gender stereotyping. In *The Voyage Out*, she charts the female rite of passage into adulthood, and explores the terror faced by a motherless girl as she approaches her moment of initiation into adult sexuality. Rachel Vinrace has no model for adult femininity/sexuality except her aunt Helen Ambrose, whose names suggest both acceptance of the male gaze and conformity to male standards and desires. In these respects, Helen anticipates some of the qualities of Mrs Ramsay in *To the Lighthouse*. Lacking the resources of Lily Briscoe, Rachel succumbs to a patriarchal system which frightens her because it seems to offer no scope for an autonomous female identity. By contrast, *Jacob's Room* explores a young man's initiation into adulthood, but from an unusual and telling perspective. Jacob's development is presented from the point of view of a series of female narrators, none of whom really understands *how* he moves with such ease into his role of dominant adult male. Jacob's self-sufficient masculinity is thus something of a puzzle to the book's narrators. The cult of masculinity is also, as in *Three Guineas*, linked with militarism and war. To a greater extent than *The Voyage Out*, *Jacob's Room* can thus be read as a punitive text.

Rachel

Rachel Vinrace of *The Voyage Out* is a young girl of twenty-four. Having lost her mother at the age of eleven, she has been brought up by two unmarried aunts who have provided her with little more stimulus than that of 'household gossip' and 'interminable walks around sheltered gardens'. She is almost completely uneducated, and knows nothing at all about sex. Her aunt Helen enlightens her with the following result:

> By this new light she saw her life for the first time a creeping, hedged-in thing, driven cautiously between high walls, here turned aside, there plunged in darkness, made dull and crippled for ever.[1]

The violence of the imagery suggests a sub-textual reference to Woolf's childhood abuse: it is also proleptic, indicating that Rachel has been *fatally* disabled by ignorance. Her journey in the novel is from innocence to a knowledge which is unbearable because it comes too late to be integrated with her experience. Her aunt, who becomes a kind of surrogate mother, explains:

> Keeping them [young girls] ignorant, of course, defeats its own object, and when they begin to understand they take it all much too seriously. (*VO*, p. 105)

The Voyage Out was conceived by Woolf not so much as a rewriting of the male *Bildungsroman* as of the male story of adventure. One of the points of the novel is

that women may grow, but they may not adventure:
only one voyage is open to them, the voyage *in* to
marriage and domesticity. Woolf makes this point
partly through her choice of textual models. *The Voyage
Out* is, as Jane Marcus has pointed out, a highly
derivative novel, but Woolf uses her models and frame
texts with the purpose of underlining significant
differences between male and female experience. For
example, as Alice Fox has shown in her meticulous
study *Virginia Woolf and the Literature of the English
Renaissance*, Elizabethan prose narratives and especially
Hakluyt's *Voyages, Travels, and Discoveries of the English
Nation* offered one important model:

> The very plot of the novel resembles countless
> narratives in Hakluyt: Rachel Vinrace journeys to
> South America on her father's ship, has a number
> of new experiences, and dies of a mysterious disease
> apparently contracted while exploring.[2]

Hakluyt does not seem at first particularly relevant to
Woolf's purposes, until we recognise that one of the
points she wishes to underscore is the world of
difference between the possibilities open to men both
in the Elizabethan period and the early twentieth
century, and those open to women. The novel shows
that over 300 years virtually no progress has been
made: Rachel is as helpless, bound and constrained as
an Elizabethan woman.

By modelling her text partly on Elizabethan colonial
narratives, Woolf is also able to make sustained use of
a metaphor which reminds us of Rachel's sexual
vulnerability. Annette Kolodny has shown that texts
from colonial periods commonly use the metaphor of
the female body to signify a new land to be entered
and conquered.[3] Woolf picks up this metaphor,

describing South America, for example, as 'a virgin land behind a veil', and throughout the text there are suggestions of an equivalence between Rachel and a new continent open to pillage and exploitation. Throughout the novel these suggestions of equivalence help to keep the ideas of invasion, plunder and even rape on the edge of consciousness.

Another text which lies 'behind' *The Voyage Out* is Conrad's *Heart of Darkness*. The textual parallels between Conrad's and Woolf's descriptions of a journey by river into an unknown land are many: more interesting are the significant configurations of the landscapes involved. John Berryman has remarked that the landscapes of Conrad's text read like sexual fantasies, governed by guilt and fear: he mentions the '*penetration*' of the Dark Continent (the mother's body)', 'a travel back in time to the womb' and 'a re-creation of a Primal Scene'.[4] *Woolf* recreates Conrad's scenes in a text which is perhaps more self-conscious but equally powerful in its use of landscape to suggest aspects of the body of woman/the body of the mother. Thus the journey up river comes to figure for Rachel primarily the frightening opening-up of her own body, while for Terence there are clearer suggestions of what Berryman calls 'a travel back in time to the womb' and to the maternal body. In the following passage, for example, we have an Oedipal journey for Terence into the 'hall' of the mother's womb:

By degrees as the river narrowed, and the high sandbanks fell to level ground thickly grown with trees, the sounds of the forest could be heard. It echoed like a hall. There were sudden cries; and then long spaces of silence, such as there are in a cathedral when a boy's voice has ceased . . . (*VO*, p. 312)

For Rachel, the journey into her own body ought,
according to conventional expectations, to be linked
with growth, but such expectations are strikingly
reversed in the text. Rachel's first sexual experience is
of Richard Dalloway's 'passionate' kiss, which is
described in terms close to those of pornography:

> Holding her tightly, he kissed her passionately, so
> that she felt the hardness of his body and the
> roughness of his cheek . . . (*VO*, p. 80)

After this experience a process of alienation and
dissociation sets in. Rachel is constantly described in
states of brooding lassitude, and becomes the prey of
illusions whereby she loses all sense of proportion. The
everyday physical objects surrounding her become
alternately tiny and irrelevant or gigantic and strange:

> She was next overcome by the unspeakable queer-
> ness of the fact that she should be sitting in an
> armchair, in the morning, in the middle of the
> world. Who were the people moving in the house –
> moving things from one place to another? And life,
> what was that? It was only a light passing over the
> surface and vanishing, as in time she would vanish,
> though the furniture in the room would remain.
> Her dissolution became so complete that she could
> not raise her finger any more, and sat perfectly still,
> listening and looking always at the same spot. It
> became stranger and stranger. She was overcome
> with awe that things should exist at all . . . She
> forgot that she had any fingers to raise . . . The
> things that existed were so immense and so desolate
> . . . (*VO*, pp. 138–9, Woolf's ellipses)

Rachel's disorder in *The Voyage Out* seems close to
hysteria, in classical Freudian terms. The hysteric,

Freud wrote, suffers from reminiscences: moreover, he argues that the structure of hysteria can be located in an attempt to return to 'the primal scenes'. It is significant that Rachel's inertia, her automaton-like state, becomes even more pronounced as she enters into a relationship with Terence Hewet which brings her closer to an understanding (which she wishes constantly to postpone) of what 'love' means. She is haunted by visions which show an awareness that for her too love must be embodied in the primal scene of penetration of the female body. This scene is apprehended in terms which suggest both horror and constraint:

> She dreamt that she was walking down a long tunnel, which grew so narrow by degrees that she could touch the damp bricks on either side. At length the tunnel opened and became a vault; she found herself trapped in it, bricks meeting her wherever she turned, alone with a little deformed man who squatted on the floor gibbering, with long nails. His face was pitted and like the face of an animal. The wall behind him oozed with damp, which collected into drops and slid down. (*VO*, p. 81)

The Voyage Out can thus be read as a first exploration, for Woolf via Rachel's consciousness, of origin and the maternal body: both are at this stage in her work seen *negatively*. In the passage quoted above the presence of the man in the woman's body is presented in terms of trauma: there is no sense here, as there will be later, of ecstasy in connexion with the (imagined) primal scene. There is a strong sense indeed of the potentially negative implications and consequences of the sexual act for women. In the passage quoted, corruption and disease are associated with it, and as Rachel later accedes to Terence (and to patriarchy), an image of churning water suggests the potentially debilitating effects of woman's reproductive life under patriarchy.

> He was afraid to kiss her again. By degrees she grew close to him and rested against him. In this position they sat for some time. She said 'Terence' once; he answered 'Rachel'.
> 'Terrible – terrible,' she murmured after another pause, but in saying this she was thinking as much of the persistent churning of the water as of her own feeling. On and on it went in the distance, the senseless and cruel churning of the water. (*VO*, p. 317)

Rachel's illness and death are explicitly connected in the text with her repudiation of sexuality. Her illness begins with a headache, of which she first becomes aware as Terence reads to her from Milton. Significantly, he is reading from *Comus* the Lady's invocation to the virgin water-nymph Sabrina, who is called on to rescue her from the dangers of the flesh represented by Comus and his magic. Woolf thus invites us to read Rachel's illness in terms of a rescue, a semi-divine intervention taking her from the dangers represented by Terence and sexuality: in her illness she imagines herself falling into a watery realm which in effect unites her with Sabrina 'under the glassy, cool, translucent wave'.

It is interesting too that as Terence reads, Rachel embarks on a particular train of thought and association. She is struck by the words 'curb', 'Locrine' and 'Brute' which bring 'unpleasant sights before her eyes' independently of their literal contextual meaning. The *associations* of these words suggest coercion, force and also some sort of threshold or dividing line ('curbing' and 'locking'). The idea of a threshold and of the loss of virginity is also suggested by Terence's response when Rachel first tells him that she has a headache:

> For a few moments they sat looking at one another in silence, holding each other's hands. During this time his sense of dismay and catastrophe were almost physically painful; all around him he seemed to hear the shiver of broken glass which, as it fell to earth, left him sitting in the open air. (*VO*, p. 381)

The breaking glass recalls the shattering of Snow White's coffin and the traditional fairy-tale kiss from the prince which also signals the loss of virginity.

The effect of all this is to suggest on the one hand that Rachel is going to escape from Terence and sexuality, while on the other we are made to feel that she has already been harmed and tampered with by him. Her illness thus comes to signify both an escape from sexuality and the damage inflicted by the sexual act as it is construed/constructed by her. The second feeling is uppermost in a striking passage in which Woolf evokes for the first time in her writing the 'primal scene' of the room and the blind which she later established in 'A Sketch of the Past' as the 'base' of her life. Here, in accordance with Rachel's repudiation of sexuality, the scene is infused with horror:

> Rachel went to bed; she lay in the dark, it seemed to her, for a very long time, but at length, waking from a transparent kind of sleep, she saw the windows white in front of her . . . Turning her eyes

to the window, she was not reassured by what she
saw there. The movement of the blind as it filled
with air and blew slowly out, drawing the cord with
a little trailing sound along the floor, seemed to her
terrifying, as if it were the movement of an animal
in the room. (*VO*, p. 382)

If the sexual scene is construed in this way, social and
cultural forces, as well as personal psychology, must
be implicated. Indeed in *The Voyage Out* Woolf is more
concerned than is often recognised with the wider
social and cultural pressures which bear on sexuality
and which can lead to its being constructed in terms of
violence/violation. She shows in this novel the all-
pervasive power and force of patriarchy and raises
many of the issues which will reappear in *A Room of
One's Own* and *Three Guineas*. One of the most
important of these is education, in a social climate
where it is possible for Hirst to ask Rachel, 'Have you
got a mind, or are you like the rest of your sex ?' It is
not just lack of education about sex, but lack of
education generally which unfits women for life
outside the domestic sphere, and which ensures that
even this life goes *unrepresented*. In a self-reflexive
passage, Woolf through Terence Hewet comments on
the ensuing difficulties for her own project of representation in the novel:

There it was going on in the background, for all
those thousands of years, this curious silent unrepresented life. Of course we're always writing
about women – abusing them, or jeering at them, or
worshipping them; but it's never come from women
themselves. I believe we still don't know in the least
how they live or what they feel, or what they do
precisely . . . But the lives of women of forty, of

unmarried women, of working women, of women who keep shops and bring up children, of women like your aunts or Mrs Thornbury or Miss Allan – one knows nothing whatever about them. (*VO*, p. 245)

Incorporating into her novel the 'unrepresented lives' of women who do not fit into a conventional romance plot, Woolf is also astute in her *qualified* use in this novel of the romance plot which formed a staple of the novel form until the twentieth century. In undermining romance in *The Voyage Out*, Woolf sharpens our awareness of its ideological function and of the inequitable social arrangements which it is designed to cover over. One of the devices Woolf uses is to parallel the Rachel–Terence romance plot with that of Susan Warrington and Arthur Venning. Because they are presented more or less in terms of caricature – Susan's breathing, for example, resembling in 'its profoundly peaceful sighs and hesitations . . . that of a cow standing up to its knees all night through in the long grass' – the crude reality of the forces which propel them into marriage can be presented with more directness than is possible with Rachel and Terence. For example, these are Susan's reflections when she becomes engaged:

Her mind, stunned to begin with, now flew to the various changes that her engagement would make – how delightful it would be to join the ranks of the married women – no longer to hang on to groups of girls much younger than herself – to escape the long solitude of an old maid's life. Now and then her amazing good fortune overcame her, and she turned to Arthur with an exclamation of love. (*VO*, p. 155)

On Susan's part, at least, the love is less real than the relief. The love betweeen Rachel and Terence also has a manufactured quality. As Avril Horner and Sue Zlosnik point out, their declarations of love seem mechanical: it is as though they are acting out predetermined roles.[5] Woolf presents 'love' in the relationship between both couples as something which is produced to fit social expectations. 'Love' must be there in order to sanctify and justify the commitment, on both sides, to a marriage contract which will secure the continued economic and social dominance of one sex over the other.

Terence and Rachel's feeling for each other is genuine, though it may not be romantic love. Nonetheless, Woolf shows that their sensations (for which, Rachel feels, there is no name, no fitting social tag) cannot possibly overcome or transcend the social pressures which have created in them deeply rooted gender-related assumptions and expectations about each other. Terence, for example, although he is used as a vehicle at one point to express Woolf's views about the position of women, is shown in a later, crucial scene to be unable to take Rachel's music seriously. While she plays a late Beethoven sonata, he comments:

> I've no objection to nice simple tunes – indeed, I find them very helpful to my literary composition, but that kind of thing is merely like an unfortunate old dog going on its hind legs in the rain. (*VO*, p. 340)

This is an indirect allusion, of course, to Dr Johnson's famous dictum that 'a woman's preaching is like a dog's walking on his hinder legs. It is not done well; but you are surprised to find it done at all'. The reference does not augur well for Terence's behaviour as a husband: it also brings the question of women and writing back to our attention, foregrounding the problems of female voice and female representation which exercise Woolf in this text.

When Woolf re-read *The Voyage Out* in 1920 she commented in her diary:

> I don't know – such a harlequinade as it is – such an assortment of patches – here simple and severe – here frivolous and shallow – here like God's truth – here strong and free flowing as I could wish.[6]

This estimate of the variegated nature of the novel has been endorsed by later critics. It seems something of a patchwork because of the number of different styles within it, encompassing social realism, satire, caricature, exotic description and inner dream-like scenes. The dream-like scenes are the freshest in the novel, for reasons which Woolf herself explored in an important passage in 'A Sketch of the Past':

> I find that scene making is my natural way of marking the past. A scene always comes to the top; arranged; representative. This confirms me in my instinctive notion – it is irrational; it will not stand argument – that we are sealed vessels afloat on what it is convenient to call reality; at some moments, without a reason, without an effort, the sealing matter cracks; in floods reality; that is a scene – for they would not survive entire so many ruinous years unless they were made of something permanent; that is a proof of their 'reality'. Is this liability to scene receiving the origin of my writing impulse?[7]

This description of a 'scene' which is 'arranged' and 'representative' is strikingly close to Freud's description of the structure of the dream in *The Interpretation of Dreams* (1900, first English translation 1913). It is of course significant, too, that Freud's dreams are *written* dreams: texts, in other words. Freud's work and the novels of Woolf may be read as inter-texts: if it is not possible to talk of direct influence, their works, nonetheless, significantly illuminate each other. It is interesting, too, that Woolf in her description of the 'scene' quoted above has recourse both to physiological and psychoanalytic terms ('sealed vessels', 'instinctive', 'irrational'). She also sketches a model of material flooding in under pressure which is very close to Freud's model of unconscious material flooding in through dream or memory, escaping censorship only because it has been 'arranged' (via condensation, displacement and secondary revision) into a manifestation or rebus which covers the latent content.

In describing these 'scenes' which she saw in 1939 as central to her writing, Woolf seems to acknowledge that they are formed in part at least through unconscious processes which work on key images and thoughts, transforming them into something which is 'arranged' for presentation to consciousness and which then has 'permanence'. Her metaphor of 'sealed vessels' (an image which had appeared earlier in *To the Lighthouse*) suggests both the fluidity of the unconscious and its power to break through the membranes of custom and censorship. The implication is that the writer must be open to such incursions: in that respect Freud's own work, with its powerful and evocative descriptions of dreams and/or remembered scenes, may have offered a model of free, 'associative' writing for Woolf. The *structure* of texts like *The Interpretation of Dreams* and Freud's case histories might also have suggested new ways in which narrative could be formed, out of loosely linked scenes or episodes interspersed with comment or analysis. It could be argued that the experimental nature of much of Woolf's fiction owed something to Freud's innovative *narrative* texts, as did that of other female modernists such as H.D., Mansfield and Sinclair.

This claim might be supported by a brief analysis of 'The Mark on the Wall', one of the early sketches (1917) which acts as a kind of template for Woolf's subsequent fiction. It is virtually a specimen piece of associative writing, structured around interlinked chains of thought. If we look briefly at the first few paragraphs, we can trace the following 'set' of images: the mark itself which might represent inauguration, difference and writing; childhood fancies about the fire, feared by Woolf; a false or fraudulent woman, dusty and bewigged; gender differentiation (woman 'pours', man 'hits'); decay and decomposition; birth/ death; rebirth and afterlife. Even through this short-hand summary, we can detect the presence of some of Woolf's fundamental themes, which seem always, as it were, to lie just beneath the surface of writing – identity and difference, gender differentiation, death and decay, redemption through connexion with the mother. The associative technique *releases* a set of ideas which is replayed with variations through the text, which goes on to explore a link between the masculine principle and death (moving through the chain of antiquary/retired Colonel/tomb/stroke), then to evoke a paradisiacal state of being which is connected with flowers, water and the presence of the mother. In a 'quiet, spacious world', the 'flowers so red and blue' representing the mother connect with a watery under-world which 'one could slice with one's thought as a fish slices the water with his fin'. It is notable that just as the flower metaphor anticipates Woolf's description of her mother in 'A Sketch of the Past', so the fish metaphor anticipates and parallels Woolf's use of it to describe female creativity in 'Professions for Women'.

Jacob

In *Jacob's Room* Woolf employs techniques developed in 'A Mark on the Wall' to explore in detail the masculine principle and the male order. But although the techniques are similar, the *problem* of representation is not. Many critics have commented on the emphasis in *Jacob's Room* on the difficulties of 'reading' – and of narrating – character. One of the most important difficulties, stressed by the narrator, is that posed by sex. How is she, a woman several years older than Jacob, both to understand him and to represent him? I want to suggest that in a sense, she cannot, and that the text charts this inability not just as part of the Modernist drift towards the destabilising of character, but as a way of further exploring the relations between gender and writing. In this novel, with its male subject, Woolf broaches the question of whether a woman's voice can speak only *of* other women *to* other women, a possibility which is hinted at in the blind woman's song:

Long past sunset an old blind woman sat on a camp-stool with her back to the stone wall of the Union of London and Smith's Bank, clasping a brown mongrel tight in her arms and singing out loud, not for coppers, no, from the depths of her gay wild heart – her sinful, tanned heart – for the child who fetches her is the fruit of sin, and should have been in bed, curtained, asleep, instead of hearing in the lamplight her mother's wild song, where she sits against the Bank, singing not for coppers, with her dog against her breast.[8]

The blind woman is heard not by Jacob but by her daughter, and her wild song, its cadences reproduced in this long rhythmical sentence, images a communication which might only be possible between women, or between mother and daughter. *Jacob's Room* is a text full of mothers and their communications; it is also full of cast-out and abandoned women whose position points up the contemporary sexual double standard. Most notable are Florinda and Fanny, Jacob's cast-offs, whose very names suggest that they are perceived and understood only in terms of sexual use.

In a striking manoeuvre, Woolf opposes these women to patriarchal *culture*, thus suggesting the ways in which 'elevated' patriarchal culture and learning are founded on a primary casting out of the material female body with its reproductive power. The oddity and the brutality of this procedure are clearly shown in the following passage:

Stone lies solid over the British Museum, as bone lies cool over the visions and heat of the brain. Only here the brain is Plato's brain and Shakespeare's; the brain has made pots and statues, great bulls and little jewels, and crossed the river of death this way and that incessantly, seeking some landing, now wrapping the body well for its long sleep; now laying a penny piece on the eyes; now turning the toes scrupulously to the East. Meanwhile, Plato continues his dialogue; in spite of the rain; in spite of the cab whistles; in spite of the woman in the mews behind Great Ormond Street who has come home drunk and cries all night long, 'Let me in! Let me in!' (*JR*, p. 149)

Plato and the woman (and later Jacob and the same woman) are pointedly juxtaposed in a passage which crystallises many of the issues Woolf was later to explore in *A Room of One's Own*. It seems likely that the woman is a prostitute: she is drunken, has no name and therefore no place in patriarchy. Cast out from the stony, bony temple of knowledge, she is connected with the other female outcasts in this text who have failed to conceal their feminine materiality beneath the veil of respectability. She joins Florinda, dismissed by Jacob because she has no mind (although she may be pregnant with some 'gentleman's' child) and Judith Shakespeare, another pregnant and anonymous woman lying 'buried at some cross-roads where the omnibuses now stop outside the Elephant and Castle'.[9]

Plato and Greek art are central to the novel. As Makiko Minow-Pinkney has pointed out, Greek civilisation was the cradle of logocentric philosophy:[10] it is perhaps appropriate then that Greek civilisation should represent an ideal for Jacob and his friends, an ideal reserved for male appreciation. Jacob leaves Florinda, on one occasion, to talk about 'something sensible' with Timmy Durrant:

They were boastful, triumphant; it seemed to both that they had read every book in the world; known every sin, passion, and joy. Civilizations stood round them like flowers ready for picking. Ages lapped at their feet like waves fit for sailing. And surveying all this, looming through the fog, the lamplight, the shades of London, the two young men decided in favour of Greece . . .

... Taking Jacob for a military gentleman, the
stall-keeper told him about his boy at Gibraltar ...
(*JR*, pp. 101–2)

In this passage, male civilisation and male hubris are
linked with potential catastrophe (we notice the
reference to 'civilizations ... ready for picking' and
the identification of Jacob as a 'military gentleman').

Jacob himself is repeatedly described in terms of
Greek art: physically he is said to resemble Greek
statues, which are presented in the text as both noble
and one-dimensional. As Jacob stands in the
Parthenon, he notices that Greek statues are un-
finished:

'And the Greeks, like sensible men, never
bothered to finish the backs of their statues,' said
Jacob, shading his eyes and observing that the side
of the figure which is turned away from view is left
in the rough. (*JR*, p. 206)

Like Jacob – and the masculine civilisation which he
represents – Greek statues can also be blind:

Sustained entirely upon picture postcards for the
past two months, Fanny's idea of Jacob was more
statuesque, noble, and eyeless than ever. To reinforce her vision she had taken to visiting the
British Museum, where, keeping her eyes downcast
until she was alongside of the battered Ulysses, she
opened them and got a fresh shock of Jacob's
presence, enough to last her half a day. (*JR*, p. 238)

Jacob's blindness – and his indifference – are contrasted with Fanny's capacities for vision and feeling.
'Rough' and 'eyeless' statues link with the series of
maimed men present in the text to suggest a masculine

culture which is monolithic and one-dimensional, to
its cost.

Jacob's Room takes its stand against classical and
masculine ideals through a double narrative move.
First, the structure of the novel is a kind of parody,
undercutting the conventional *Bildungsroman*, the novel
of male development and identity. As many critics
have pointed out, the novel refuses to recognise and
give proper weight to what are commonly held to be
the turning points in a young man's development –
going to school, going up to university, finding a
profession and a way in the world, for example. Such
incidents are referred to only in passing in *Jacob's
Room*, and instead there are a series of displacements
whereby a holiday in Cornwall, a Guy Fawkes party, a
trip to Paris and then to Greece, form the narrative
centres of the text. This of course makes it a more
conventionally 'feminine' novel, in the sense that the
focus is on Jacob's emotional life, on encounters in the
social world, and on relations between the sexes.
Rather than charting a young girl's progress from one
suitor to the next, we thus follow Jacob's relations
with Clara, with Florinda and with Sandra
Wentworth-Williams.

There is, then, a shift in the centre of gravity of the
novel, a move to the feminine sphere. This in itself has
marked the novel as 'feminine' for some critics: it has
been suggested by Bowlby, for example, that Jacob's
story is told from the point of view of the woman as
outsider, removed both from male rites of passage and
from the narrative conventions governing their representation.[11] More radically and specifically, it could be
argued that Woolf's strategy in this novel is to oppose
male forms of representation by creating a text woven,
paradoxically, out of what she calls 'the unpublished
works of women' (*JR*, p. 123).

The novel begins with one of Betty Flanders's letters:

> 'So of course,' wrote Betty Flanders, pressing her heels rather deeper in the sand, 'there was nothing for it but to leave.'
>
> Slowly welling from the point of her gold nib, pale blue ink dissolved the full stop; for there her pen stuck; her eyes fixed, and tears slowly filled them. The entire bay quivered; the lighthouse wobbled; and she had the illusion that the mast of Mr Connor's little yacht was bending like a wax candle in the sun. She winked quickly. Accidents were awful things. She winked again. The mast was straight; the waves were regular; the lighthouse was upright; but the blot had spread. (*JR*, p. 3)

The regular march of proper syntax is linked here with a male-centred, phallocratic world, complete with mast and lighthouse. Betty's writing, by contrast, is linked with bodily fluids (tears, and by implication milk): it wells and dissolves organised syntax just as her tears dissolve perspective. This feminine writing, 'many-paged, tear-stained' both opens the text and licenses its procedures: like this letter, the text of *Jacob's Room* will be composed from a fluctuating, multiple point of view, with constant shifts in time and tense, without regard for conventional narrative order. From the beginning of the text, Woolf valorises this multiple, 'feminine' creativity,[12] this ability to create a mosaic of meaning and to hold different perspectives together, without regard for the expected. Of Betty the narrator asks:

> Who shall deny that this blankness of mind, when combined with profusion, mother wit, old wives'

tales, haphazard ways, moments of astonishing
daring, humour and sentimentality – who shall
deny that in these respects every woman is nicer
than any man? (*JR*, p. 9)

'Mother wit' is important: repeatedly the narrator
refers to Betty's motherly characteristics and their
translation into her writing – to Mr Floyd's proposal
of marriage, for example, Betty returns 'such a
motherly, respectful, inconsequent, regretful letter
that he kept it for many years'.

Later, the narrator describes Betty's letters to
Jacob:

and how interesting her letters were, about Mrs
Jarvis, could one read them year in, year out – the
unpublished works of women, written by the
fireside in pale profusion, dried by the flame, for the
blotting-paper's worn to holes and the nib cleft and
clotted. (*JR*, 122–3)

Jacob's Room provides us with something close to
Betty's letters through the apparent vagaries of its
own textual procedures and through its associative,
multiple quality. It also provides us with a narrative
which is almost entirely constructed by women. The
narrator, as has been pointed out, foregrounds her sex
and the possible difficulties of interpretation which
may ensue. Frequently – as in all Woolf's texts – she
merges with the characters, and these are nearly all
women, to the extent that the narrative of *Jacob's Room*
could be said to be carried by a confederacy of women,
murmuring and conferring about him. We learn about
Jacob from Clara Durrant, from Florinda and Fanny;
also from mothers like Mrs Norman, at one end of the
social scale, who compares Jacob with her own son,

and Mrs Papworth from the other, a mother of nine who preserves a sceptical distance from Jacob's invocation of the 'good' and of 'absolute' truth (*JR*, p. 138).

Jacob is thus presented from an almost exclusively feminine perspective, in a text where the techniques of gossip and letter writing are privileged over conventional narrative and its orders. Woolf stresses the dangers of her method in *Jacob's Room*, her anxiety over the fact that she is turning to a kind of writing which traditionally perishes rather than endures, but she emphasises too the strength of the female tradition of mother-wit and mother-writing with which she wishes to align herself:

> The words we seek hang close to the tree. We come at dawn and find them sweet beneath the leaf.
>
> Mrs Flanders wrote letters; Mrs Jarvis wrote them; Mrs Durrant too; Mother Stuart actually scented her pages, thereby adding a flavour which the English language fails to provide ... (*JR*, pp. 126–7)

Woolf's identification with a feminine perspective, as well as with a feminine writing physically marked with its material origin, is a crucial factor in the presentation of Jacob's 'character'. Jacob's opacity, his lack of character in the traditional sense, has often been related to Woolf's theories about fictional character as they are set out in 'Modern Fiction' and 'Mr Bennett and Mrs Brown', or to her interest in contemporary Post-Impressionist painting technique. More recently, critics have interpreted Jacob's 'emptiness' in terms of a Derridean 'break' between sign and origin[13] or the general problem of the relation between individual and type.[14] However, it is also possible to read the narrator's difficulty with Jacob in terms of the problematic of sexual difference. As the narrator suggests, using the metaphor of landscape painting, the 'effect of sex' in matters of representation is to alter focus and perspective. It can also, it appears, make the object in view seem 'wavy, tremulous' (reminding us again perhaps of Betty Flanders's tears). The waviness, the indistinctness, the 'blur' (a word used repeatedly in connection with Jacob), are perhaps the marks both of the suspension of dominant (male) codes of representation and of the privileging of subjective impression over the objectivity which Woolf associates with Greek (male) art. The problem is particularly acute when a woman artist takes a male subject. Jacob's maleness entails, from the perspective of this narrator, a self-sufficiency which closes him off from view and from her interpretation. He is, as it were, a subject without a predicate, without apparent *need* of a predicate. If, as Gayatri Spivak suggests, *To the Lighthouse* involves precisely the investigation of what Mrs Ramsay 'is', so that the novel is structured like a sentence with a changing predicate,[12] *Jacob's Room* has a subject which literally cannot be articulated by its narrator. Jacob 'is', so to speak, nothing: or, self-reflexively, Jacob 'is' Jacob. It is Jacob's self-sufficiency which removes him from the sphere of this narrative's interpretation or explanation and this self-sufficiency is, in turn, shown to be the 'natural' result of centuries of patriarchal dominance. Jacob himself feels no need to justify or prove himself, for his place or 'room' within the house of patriarchy is guaranteed:

> Was it to receive this gift from the past that the young man came to the window and stood there, looking out across the court? It was Jacob. He stood smoking his pipe while the last stroke of the clock

purred softly round him. Perhaps there had been an argument. He looked satisfied; indeed masterly; which expression changed slightly as he stood there, the sound of the clock conveying to him (it may be) a sense of old buildings and time; and himself the inheritor. (*JR*, p. 57)

Indeed, Jacob's collusion with patriarchy is underscored in the text, and our awareness of this modifies and tempers our response to his death. Jacob, the son who is killed, is the only one of Betty Flanders's sons 'who never obeyed her': wilfully he strays from her influence and is connected with a disturbing violence which seems to come 'naturally' to him. Jacob has no father to instruct him in the arts of hunting and killing; nonetheless he is twice associated with violence and with 'death in the forest' in the early part of the novel. His response to the 'primal scene' of the 'enormous man and woman' stretched out on the beach is one of distress deflected by his discovery of the sheep's skull. He runs away with this, clasping it to his chest, the implication being that he has somehow allied himself with a principle of destruction. The motif of the skull recurs in the narrator's stylised (and repeated) description of Jacob's rooms in London – 'over the doorway a rose, or a ram's skull, is carved in the wood'. This image occurs too in *To the Lighthouse* where, Mary Jacobus suggests[16] the boar's skull may figure both the phallus and the possibility of fetishising it. In *Jacob's Room* the suggestion is less of fetishisation than of a sublimation of male energy creating the 'unseizable force' which 'oars the world forward'. The possibility of 'reading' the carving as a 'multifoliate rose' suggests the alternative possibilities of female sexuality, denied and/or repressed by Jacob.

The text emphasises, shockingly, the complicity of young men with the patriarchal order which holds them in place as subjects. We can see this clearly by juxtaposing two passages from the novel. The first comes from the description of a service in King's College Chapel:

> Look, as they pass into service, how airily the gowns blow out, as though nothing dense and corporeal were within. What sculptured faces, what certainty, authority controlled by piety, although great boots march under the gowns. In what orderly procession they advance. Thick wax candles stand upright; young men rise in white gowns; while the subservient eagle bears up for inspection the great white book. (*JR*, p. 38)

The second runs as it were in counterpoint:

> The battleships ray out over the North Sea, keeping their stations accurately apart. At a given signal all the guns are trained on a target which (the master gunner counts the seconds, watch in hand – at the sixth he looks up) flames into splinters. With equal nonchalance a dozen young men in the prime of life descend with composed faces into the depths of the sea; and there impassively (though with perfect mastery of machinery) suffocate uncomplainingly together. (*JR*, p. 216)

The first passage is proleptic in a covert way.: we can choose to read it in a double fashion, focusing for example on the punning ambiguity of the word 'service', connoting religious and/or military service. The 'great boots' also point forward to the war, while mention of the 'great white book' of the Bible serves to yoke together religious and military spheres, the one legitimating and supporting the other. The 'certainty' and 'authority' of the young men depend too on denial of the material body (with its implication of origin in the maternal body): 'airily' the flesh must be denied in the pursuit of transcendence (compare Jacob's rejection of the 'fleshy . . . damned women' who threaten his appreciation of Greek art, p. 143). The unity and the passivity ('subservience') of the young men are also evident in this passage.

In the second passage the young men have the same 'certainty' and 'authority', here translated as 'mastery'. They have the same unity, and frightening passivity ('impassively', 'uncomplainingly'). The text thus seems to suggest that their fall into the material/maternal sea is the necessary consequence of their earlier pride and inertia – which the reader links, of course, with that of Jacob, whose unthinking self-sufficiency has been noted above.

Jacob's Room thus constitutes a critique of masculinity as the norm of a culture in which maleness automatically guarantees the authenticity and authority of the subject. With its slant-eyed view of Jacob, and its destabilising of the expected balance of the text (the subject of the novel is not Jacob, but women's experience of him), the novel anticipates many of the concerns and techniques of *A Room of One's Own*, a text with which it is closely linked. *Jacob's Room* gives us a multiple perspective on Jacob via a series of female voices: these are often presented in non-standard English and in non-standard literary forms. To this extent Woolf is anticipating the project called for in *A Room of One's Own*: a rewriting of history from the point of view of women, a reinstatement of the female point of view, using forms which are 'proper for (women's) own use'. *Jacob's Room* is also tied to *A Room of One's Own* through imagery: the first half of *A Room of One's Own* recapitulates and builds on many of the central images of *Jacob's Room* (Cambridge, presented from the outside; the British Museum, ditto; the stories of Fanny and Florinda, exiles from culture and language). The overlapping of the two texts is significant: it suggests the permeability of the barrier between fiction and essay-writing for Woolf.

Jacob's Room is a novel in which Woolf may seem to come close to essentialism. As we have seen, the qualities of violence in Jacob are presented as 'natural' or inherent: there is little emphasis on growth or change in his character. The virtue of Betty Flanders is similarly taken as given, and there is no prolonged investigation of the cultural determinants of her admirable 'feminine' qualities. But the effectiveness of the text is in part the result of this simple, diagrammatic quality. The primary 'scene' behind the text is that of the son escaping the mother: this is embedded deeply within the text, motivating the narrative even through such apparent diversions as the description of Mrs Pascoe's cottage in Chapter 4:

> Although it would be possible to knock at the cottage door and ask for a glass of milk, it is only thirst that would compel the intrusion. Yet perhaps Mrs Pascoe would welcome it. The summer's day may be wearing heavy. Washing in her little scullery, she may hear the cheap clock on the mantelpiece tick, tick, tick . . . tick, tick, tick. She is alone in the house. Her husband is out helping Father Hosken; her daughter married and gone to America. Her elder son is married, too, but she does not agree with his wife. The Wesleyan minister came along and took the younger boy. She is alone in the house. (*JR*, p. 68)

Mrs Pascoe can be read as another of the avatars of Betty Flanders, a mother from whom Jacob will not take milk on his journey in Cornwall, just as he will not take nurture or advice from his own mother. The parallel with Betty gives substance and point to one of the many detours through the consciousness of mothers in the text.

To be able to stand in the place of the mother is important for the narrator of this text. In *Jacob's Room* Woolf moves from the relatively impersonal narrative stance of *The Voyage Out* and *Night and Day* to take up a narrative position which is aligned with the view(s) of the mothers in the text. It is a position self-consciously adopted, and the text at times comes close to parody of female/maternal characteristics. Nonetheless, through Betty Flanders Woolf is able to loosen up her narrative voice, to shape it to her own use. Betty also offers a model of sustained creativity which is conspicuously independent of the male, and associated with close relations between women:

> Mrs Flanders liked Mrs Jarvis, always said of her that she was too good for such a quiet place, and, though she never listened to her discontent and told her at the end of it (looking up, sucking her thread, or taking off her spectacles) that a little peat wrapped round the iris roots keeps them from the frost ... Mrs Flanders knew precisely how Mrs Jarvis felt. (*JR*, p. 122)

These elements of *Jacob's Room* are developed further in *Mrs Dalloway* and *To the Lighthouse*, both of which, of course, have mothers as central characters.

3 Romancing the Feminine: *Mrs Dalloway* and *To the Lighthouse*

Mrs Dalloway

In *Mrs Dalloway*, the traces remain of the female collectivity of authorship of *Jacob's Room*. In the opening sections, the consciousness of Mrs Dalloway is linked with that of a series of other women (nearly all mothers) through the image of the rose, which functions frequently in Woolf's writing as an image of female sexuality and creativity. These women have little in common save their possession of this image/emblem, which is given a distinctive stamp, nonetheless, in connexion with each. Mrs Dalloway's roses are viewed by her in terms which anticipate our knowledge of her narrow bed and 'tight stretched' sheets – 'how fresh, like frilled linen clean from a laundry laid in wicker trays, the roses looked'.[1] The roses of the prostitute 'Shawled Moll Pratt' are in contrast equated with 'the price of a pot of beer' (*MD*, p. 23), while working-class Mrs Dempster craves 'the kiss of pity' from a young girl in compensation for her loss of attractiveness and sensuality:

> For it's been a hard life, thought Mrs Dempster. What hadn't she given to it? Roses; figure; her feet too. (She drew the knobbed lumps beneath her skirt.)

Roses, she thought sardonically. All trash, m'dear. (*MD*, p. 35)

As each woman's interpretation and use of her sexual identity necessarily differs, so too does her perspective on the 'reality' presented to us in the novel. More emphatically than *Jacob's Room*, *Mrs Dalloway* requires the reader to adjust his/her interpretive strategies in view of the multivalence of the narrative point of view. The narrative technique is that of multiselective omniscience, in which a single narrator, omniscient and impersonal, uses their omniscience in order to report, and sometimes to convey almost literally, the thoughts and impressions of a given character. In each sequence of the narrative, the focus is on a single character who then becomes the 'reflector' of the text. However, the narrative seldom remains straightforwardly within that single character's perspective, but moves fluidly between characters:

And this has been going on all the time! he thought; week after week; Clarissa's life; while I – he thought; and at once everything seemed to radiate from him; journeys; rides; quarrels; adventures; bridge parties; love affairs; work; work, work! and he took out his knife quite openly – his old horn-handled knife *which Clarissa could swear he had had these thirty years* – and clenched his fist upon it. (*MD*, p. 56)

The effect of this is not just to create a smooth transition (here, to Clarissa's point of view), nor simply to emphasise the fragility of subjective constructions of reality (we notice here the contrast between Peter's linear construction of the lives of others and his sense of his own life as a circle or globe).

The movements between characters, and elsewhere in the text between focalised narrative and passages of omniscient description or commentary, also make it difficult for the reader to locate the source of any given thought or construction of 'reality' in the text. This in turn calls into question the usefulness of the category of the 'character', or autonomous 'full' subject, for the reader of *Mrs Dalloway*.

Such an undermining of the notion of the autonomous subject is, it could be argued, reinforced by the use of the same narrative voice across most (though not all) of the text. Many critics have commented adversely on this feature of Woolf's novels, seeing it as the result of a failure to acknowledge the 'otherness' of existence outside a particular circle and class. Yet, as Daniel Ferrer suggests, this uniformity could be seen not as refusal of otherness, but as acceptance, a refusal to reduce the speech of the 'other' to, as he puts it, 'linguistic curiosities in relation to the speech of the author'. For Ferrer, this has the result that in Woolf's texts:

> This surface equality, this absence of rupture, means that the troubling of enunciation which occurs at one point may well extend to the whole.[2]

In turn, we might want to relate this 'troubling of enunciation', this disturbance of relations, to what Cixous would call a 'feminine' economy at work in Woolf's texts, which continually move towards an effacement of the constituted subject, an emptying of the 'full' self in order that the other should be known. The project of the fiction could thus be described as that of creating a subject which would always be exposed and traversed by 'the other'.

We might find a metaphor for this project in

Woolf's description of the old woman singing outside Regent's Park Tube in *Mrs Dalloway*. Significantly, this song is presented at first as sexless, just as a 'feminine' economy is in principle sexless, available to both male and female subjects. The old woman's voice is 'of no age or sex': she is clearly beyond sexuality in terms of its defining her social use and function. Yet the singer (the only real representative of the artist in this text, clearly linked with the old blind woman in *Jacob's Room*) still happens, by chance, to be a woman, marked by the cultural signs of difference ' – for she wore a skirt –' (*MD*, p. 106). The song is initially described as 'having no human meaning': it is a collocation of meaningless syllables from which syntax has been obliterated, depriving us of any sense of the ordered relations of subject and predicate. It has no purpose, 'bubbling up without direction', and yet partakes of eternity, moaning in 'the eternal breeze'. We are given this information through the consciousness of Peter Walsh, but then there is a dislocation in the narrative of a type which is relatively frequent in *Mrs Dalloway*. The narrative shifts away from the characters and asserts a knowledge which it cannot logically have, as the narrator moves into an exaggerated fantasy about the song, inventing or finding a meaning where earlier there was none to be discerned:

> Through all ages – when the pavement was grass, when it was swamp, through the age of tusk and mammoth, through the age of silent sunrise – the battered woman – for she wore a skirt – with her right hand exposed, her left clutching at her side, stood singing of love – love which has lasted a million years, she sang, love which prevails, and millions of years ago her lover, who had been dead

these centuries, had walked, she crooned, with her
in May; but in the course of ages, long as summer
days, and flaming, she remembered, with nothing
but red asters, he had gone; death's enormous sickle
had swept those tremendous hills, and when at last
she laid her hoary and immensely aged head on the
earth, now become a mere cinder of ice, she
implored the Gods to lay by her side a bunch of
purple heather, there on her high burial place
which the last rays of the last sun caressed; for then
the pageant of the universe would be over. (*MD*,
pp. 105–6)

This passage has a curious status, analogous to that of
many in Woolf's non-fictional texts, particularly *A
Room of One's Own*. It is as though Woolf has recourse
to a particular kind of fantasy when she wants to write
about areas of human experience, for example sexual
difference, where it is in the nature of the subject that
there can be no final agreement, security or certainty
of 'truth'. The *suggestion* in this passage is that the song
of this 'person who happens to be a woman' is eternal,
associated with 'all ages' in the 'pageant of the
universe': it is also connected with origins, though the
evolutionary allusions to swamp and mammoth, and
also the metaphors of the spring and the pump – in the
next paragraph the song is described as 'bubbling'
and 'streaming' over the pavement, 'fertilizing,
leaving a damp stain'. A woman's song, and by
implication, women's art, are thus metaphorically
connected with an originating creative principle: thus,
again by indirection, Woolf can be seen to be
contesting the creative dominance of men, their
exclusive association with creativity.

The old woman 'croons' of a love which moves
through and across ages, in which the *identity* of the

lovers is unimportant: to this extent this love is trans-personal, non-narcissistic:

> remembering how once she had walked in May, where the sea flows now, with whom it did not matter . . . (*MD*, p. 107)

It is a love within which appropriation and specular-isation are absent, and it is connected, significantly, not with the gaze, but with touch:

> She no longer saw brown eyes, black whiskers or sunburnt face, but only a looming shape . . . to which, with the bird-like freshness of the very aged, she still twittered 'give me your hand and let me press it gently'. (p. 91)

The old woman's love song might be read as an image of love in a 'feminine economy', as Cixous describes it. She is associated with Clarissa, as we shall see: they are metaphorically linked in that the old woman is described as 'a rusty pump' 'a funnel', while Clarissa is connected in the memory of Peter Walsh with a broken but endlessly streaming fountain:

> The fountain was in the middle of a little shrubbery, far from the house, with shrubs and trees all round it. There she came, even before the time, and they stood with the fountain between them, the spout (it was broken) dribbling water incessantly. How sights fix themselves upon the mind! For example, the vivid green moss. (*MD*, p. 83)

The emphasis in this passage, and in that describing the old woman, on the 'feminine' element of water, and on fertility, is of course important – 'the vivid green moss'.

The old woman is connected through narrative perspective with Peter Walsh, who, interestingly, perceives his relation to her in terms of the economics of patriarchal society – he gives her a coin. Rezia Warren Smith notices her, identifies with a plight which she connects with weakness of gender ('Suppose one's father, or somebody who had known one in better days had happened to pass' . . .) and is finally soothed by her song ('this old woman singing . . . made her suddenly quite sure that everything was going to be right) (p. 108). The old woman does not, on the other hand, impinge at all on the consciousness of Septimus Warren Smith, a character for whom the relations between subject and object have become destabilised.

It has been traditional in Woolf criticism to see Septimus as a rather romantic 'double' for Clarissa, and recently, too, Minow-Pinkney has described the relation between the two characters as follows:

> The invention of Septimus is thus a defensive 'splitting', whereby Clarissa's most dangerous impulses are projected into another figure who can die for her; to this extent, she and he are one composite character.[3]

It could be argued, however, that this is to give the link between Clarissa and Septimus the wrong kind of emphasis. Rather than seeing the two characters as complementary, it is possible to see Septimus more negatively as embodying aspects of a masculinity foreign to Clarissa, to which she is opposed.

This is not, of course, to suggest that Septimus is a character whom we view without sympathy. To a certain extent *Mrs Dalloway* is a reparative text in that it rewrites the story of Jacob via that of Septimus, returning to the question of male complicity with the patriarchal social order which 'produced' the First World War. Septimus, however, comes from a different social class from Jacob, and is presented as having a much more 'feminine' nature, initially. The war appears to change this:

> Septimus was one of the first to volunteer. He went to France to save an England which consisted almost entirely of Shakespeare's plays and Miss Isobel Pole in a green dress walking in a square. There in the trenches the change which Mr Brewer desired when he advised football was produced instantly; he developed manliness; he was promoted; he drew the attention, indeed the affection of his officer, Evans by name. (*MD*, p. 112)

It is significant that in acquiring 'manliness' Septimus also acquires a male object of love. His relationship with Evans is described as follows:

> It was a case of two dogs playing on a hearthrug; one worrying a paper screw, snarling, snapping, giving a pinch, now and then, at the old dog's ear; the other lying somnolent, blinking at the fire, raising a paw, turning and growling good-temperedly. They had to be together, share with each other, fight with each other, quarrel with each other. (*MD*, p. 112)

'Manliness', in other words, is secured for Septimus through his identification with Evans, in a same-sex relation which emphasises sameness rather than difference. Septimus is able to carry on after the war only to the extent that he refuses to accept Evans's death, and the fact that 'here was the end of a friendship' which had provided a narcissistic mirroring of 'masculine' characteristics. Difference makes its call on Septimus through the reappearances of Evans, which figure transgression and the rupturing of the boundaries between life and death. However, Septimus cannot countenance difference and the *suspension* of identity which is called for in the recognition of otherness. (Compare Woolf on the 'psychological sentence of the feminine gender' which is 'capable of stretching to the extreme, of *suspending* the frailest particles'.[4]) Instead he reads all marks of difference in terms of a threat to his beleaguered identity:

> [Human beings] hunt in packs. Their packs scour the desert and vanish screaming into the wilderness. They desert the fallen. They are plastered over with grimaces. There was Brewer at the office, with his waxed moustache, coral tie-pin, white slip, and pleasurable emotions – all coldness and clamminess within . . . or Amelia Whatshername, handing round cups of tea punctually at five – a leering, sneering, obscene little harpy. (*MD*, p. 117)

As the passage continues Septimus goes on to condemn a 'maimed file of lunatics' for 'apologetically, yet triumphantly' inflicting their woes on others, without his being aware that such infliction is precisely the mode of his own relation to Rezia. Septimus's egotism and the insecurity which conditions it are, however, very closely linked in this text with social class. For example, the fact that Clarissa and Septimus share a quotation from *Cymbeline* ('Fear no more the heat o' the sun') only serves to underline the vast disparity in their relation to dominant culture. Septimus wants to be a writer, yet this ambition is compromised by his social class, or more precisely by his existing on the borders between the working class and the middle class:

> He was, on the whole, a border case, neither one thing nor the other . . . one of those half-educated, self-educated men whose education is all learnt from books borrowed from public libraries, read in the evening after the day's work, on the advice of well-known authors consulted by letter. (*MD*, p. 109)

Woolf emphasises the barriers which prevent Septimus's having an automatic access to culture and an automatic (almost unconscious) sense of himself as a full, bourgeois subject. The contrast with Jacob will be readily apparent.

Septimus's insecurities and 'feminine' characteristics are masked by a cultivated assertiveness and self-centredness. Perhaps it is not surprising, then, that in his experience of hallucination, Septimus sees the outside world anthropomorphically, as an extension of himself:

> But they beckoned; leaves were alive; trees were alive. And the leaves being connected by millions of fibres with his own body, there on the seat, fanned it up and down; when the branch stretched he, too, made that statement. (*MD*, p. 28)

He suffers from the delusion that he is Christ, and thinks of himself as 'the greatest of mankind' and as a 'scapegoat', both suffering for others and being 'called forth in advance of the mass of men' to 'hear the truth'. These delusions precede a suicide about which the text is ambivalent. Septimus's leap through the window could be seen as an act of phallic self-assertion, conterminous with the kind of 'masculine' egotism and assertiveness drawn from him by the experience of war:

> Coming down the staircase opposite an old man stopped and stared at him. Holmes was at the door. 'I'll give it you!' he cried, and flung himself vigorously, violently down on to Mrs Filmer's area railings. (*MD*, p. 195)

As Sue Roe has pointed out, the suicide's gesture of self-effacement is 'perhaps the most ambiguous it is ever possible to make'.[5] Clarissa's response to the news of Septimus's suicide contains and reproduces this ambivalence. The text deploys two metaphors at this point which were earlier associated with Clarissa's love for Sally Seaton: that of closeness/rapture ('some pressure of rapture . . . the close withdrew') and that of treasure ('a diamond, something infinitely precious'). The later passage runs as follows:

> Death was defiance. Death was an attempt to communicate, people feeling the impossibility of reaching the centre which, mystically, evaded them: *closeness drew apart; rapture faded*; one was alone. There was an embrace in death.
>   But this young man who had killed himself – had he plunged holding *his treasure*? 'If it were now to die, 'twere now to be most happy,' she had said to herself once, coming down, in white. (*MD*, pp. 241–2)

'Rapture' and 'closeness' in the earlier passage figure *jouissance*, or the intimacy which is knowledge, to borrow terms from *To the Lighthouse*. Failing the

achievement of this closeness, Clarissa's later meditation seems to imply, Septimus has plunged to his
death with his treasure intact, a treasure which it is
tempting to read as a metaphor for the self. The
retention of the 'self' has its positive aspects: Septimus
keeps his integrity. But he also retains his egotism, the
shell or carapace which prevents any relation with 'the
other'. Clarissa's development in the text is in the
opposite direction.

Clarissa's sense of self is a 'gift' from Sally Seton, in
a relationship which is *not* one of narcissistic mirroring. Her gift or treasure is significantly not to be
looked at, not to be deliberately regarded. It comes
from and moves within, Cixous might argue, a
'feminine' economy of 'depropriation' : it is to be kept
but not thought of or measured in terms of its
'exchange value':

> And she felt that she had been given a present,
> wrapped up, and told just to keep it, not to look at it
> – a diamond, something infinitely precious,
> wrapped up, which, as they walked (up and down,
> up and down), she uncovered, or the radiance
> burnt through, the revelation, the religious feeling!
> (*MD*, pp. 45–6)

Paradoxically, such a sense of self necessarily has
inscribed within it the possibility of loss. A 'depropriative' economy resists the temptations of holding
and fixing, moving towards flux rather than rigidity.
Not more than two pages on in the text, we have a
representation of the now middle-aged Clarissa as a
dispersed and split subject:

> How many million times she had seen her face,
> and always with the same imperceptible contrac-
> tion! She pursed her lips when she looked in the

glass. It was to give her face point. That was herself
– pointed; dart-like; definite. That was herself when
some effort, some call on her to be herself, drew the
parts together, she alone knew how different, how
incompatible and composed so for the world only
into one centre, one diamond. (*MD*, pp. 47–8)

Clarissa sees the self as crossed and split: multiple,
only artificially pulled together into a semblance of
harmony for social purposes. Significantly, Clarissa is
shown constructing herself as an (apparently) unified
subject in front of the mirror. Narcissism underwrites
the production of a fixed, coherent self ('she . . . had
tried to be the same always'), but the text increasingly
emphasises the discrepancy between this appearance
and reality. Clarissa uses the same metaphor as Mrs
Ramsay to gesture to the gap between conscious and
unconscious life ('our apparitions . . . are so moment-
ary compared with the other, the unseen part of us,
which spreads wide'), and, increasingly, we are aware
of Clarissa's moving towards a disassembling of her
'self', nowhere more so than at her party. Paradoxically, Clarissa must 'unself' herself for this social
occasion, yielding to the pressure of difference, if she is
to create a sea-changed medium in which others (and
their otherness) can flourish:

It marked a stage, this post that she felt herself to
have become, for oddly enough she had quite
forgotten what she looked like, but felt herself a
stake driven in at the top of the stairs. Every time
she gave a party she had this feeling of being
something not herself, and that everyone was
unreal in one way; much more real in another. It
was, she thought, partly their clothes, partly being
taken out of their ordinary ways, partly the

background; it was possible to say things you couldn't say anyhow else, things that needed an effort; possible to go much deeper. (*MD*, pp. 223–4)

It is at the party, too, that Clarissa's mother is mentioned, for the first and only time. Clarissa is compared to her mother by Mrs Hilbery, emerging from *Night and Day*, and at this her eyes 'filled with tears'. The metaphor of water seeps into the description of Clarissa in her 'mermaid's dress' at the party:

She wore ear-rings, and a silver-green mermaid's dress. Lolloping on the waves and braiding her tresses she seemed, having that gift still; to be; to exist; to sum it all up in the moment as she passed; turned, caught her scarf in some other woman's dress, unhitched it, laughed, all with the most perfect ease and air of a creature floating in its element. But age had brushed her; even as a mermaid might behold in her glass the setting sun on some very clear evening over the waves. There was a breath of tenderness; her severity, her prudery, her woodenness were all warmed through now. (*MD*, p. 228)

The watery metaphors suggest the 'feminine' aspects of Clarissa's responsiveness to others, her ability to merge together the people inhabiting the space of her party. It is important to stress, too, that the ability 'to be . . . to sum it all up', recognised by Peter Walsh, is not at all the attribute of a stable character – 'the old, stable ego of the character' as Lawrence has it. Clarissa is able 'to be' only because she is willing also continually to let go, living from discontinuous moment to moment, without attempting to fix identity or pleasure.

Despite the air of 'virginity' which marks Clarissa in relation to her husband, she is capable of being 'warmed through' by 'something central which permeated, something warm which broke up surfaces', in her relations with women. Clarissa is capable of strong erotic feelings for other women: there is no reason to avoid the word lesbian in describing these attachments, for they are specifically of the body, and erotic. Yet it is also true that in Woolf's fiction in general, same-sex relationships offer the chance of a redefinition of subjectivity which is not *necessarily* dependent on erotic relation. Same-sex relationships are necessarily constituted through both identity and difference, or identification and detachment. They offer an image for a relation to the other based on a non-exclusive sense of difference: as Clarissa puts it in thinking of her relation with Sally, 'it was completely disinterested', unmarked by the appropriative and possessive elements which characterise relations between men and women in patriarchy. The primary model for such a relation is of course that with the mother, and the traces of that origin remain in the text's description of Clarissa's feelings for women. These are always stimulated by 'a woman, not a girl' confessing some sexual 'scrape' or 'folly':

> It was a sudden revelation, a tinge like a blush which one tried to check and then, as it spread, one yielded to its expansion, and rushed to the farthest verge and there quivered and felt the world come closer, swollen with some astonishing significance, some pressure of rapture, which split its thin skin and gushed and poured with an extraordinary alleviation over the cracks and sores. Then, for that moment, she had seen an illumination; a match burning in a crocus; an inner meaning almost

expressed. But the close withdrew; the hard softened. It was over – the moment. (*MD*, p. 41)

Although it is possible to read this passage as 'phallic',[6] it is also possible to see it as suggestive of female orgasm ('blush', 'spread', 'expansion', 'rushed', 'quivered') and of female creativity and childbirth ('swollen', 'split', 'gushed', 'poured'). The powerful image of liquid pouring over and alleviating 'cracks and sores' suggests the healing power of the mother (who may heal over and close up the 'crack' of sexual difference). It may also of course refer further back still to the mother's feeding of the child, which constitutes the primary 'alleviation', of hunger.

Woolf here inextricably links desire, women's feeling for other women, and the memory of the mother. She thus aligns herself, through Clarissa, with 'feminine' structures of relationship, and also with a primary maternal principle of creativity. As Marianne Hirsch points out, Woolf was part of a generation of women writers for whom it was important to re-emphasise the creative power of the mother.[7] It could indeed be argued that one of the most striking features of twentieth-century aesthetics has been the casting and typing of artistic creativity in terms of sexual difference and sexual relations.[8] It is interesting to trace the pattern of male affirmation in, for example, the writings of D.H. Lawrence and Wyndham Lewis, and to contrast it with the affirmation of female creativity by their contemporaries, Woolf and Katherine Mansfield. We can see a related struggle being carried out in the psychoanalytic field in the work of Freud, on the one hand, and Melanie Klein on the other. Klein's essay 'Envy and Gratitude' contains a passage which, with its emphasis on female creativity holding off the breach of death, might serve as a final gloss on *Mrs Dalloway*:

> The 'good' breast that feeds and initiates the love relation to the mother is the representative of the life instinct and is also felt as the *first manifestation of creativeness*. In this fundamental relation the infant receives not only the gratification he [sic] desires but feels that he is being kept alive. For hunger, which rouses the fear of starvation . . . is felt as the threat of death.[9]

To the Lighthouse

In *To the Lighthouse* the connexion between the mother's absence and the 'threat of death' is, of course, fully explored. Melanie Klein's views on the developing relationship between the young girl and her mother are illuminating in connection with the treatment of this theme in *To the Lighthouse*. In an essay of 1929,[10] Klein argued that the most profound anxiety experienced by the young girl stemmed from an infantile desire to rob the mother's body of its contents, a desire which provoked anxiety that the mother would in her turn rob the child's body of its contents, destroying or mutilating her. Only the presence of the real, loving mother could, she argued, diminish the dread of the terrifying mother, whose introjected image remained in the child's mind. At a later stage, Klein suggested, the content of the dread changed from that of an attacking mother to the fear that 'the real, loving mother may be lost and that the girl will be left solitary and forsaken'.[11]

Klein illustrated her theory with reference to the development of a woman painter, Ruth Kjar. Klein notes that Kjar was first stimulated to paint by the existence of an empty space on the walls of her home, a space which 'seemed to coincide with the empty space within her'. Klein further remarks on the filling of the 'empty space' with pictures of Kjar's mother, in one painting old and disillusioned, in another 'slim, imperious, challenging'. Relating the 'empty space' to the sense of identity and the complex mirroring which goes on between mother and daughter, Klein then goes on to offer the following interpretation of the paintings:

It is obvious that the desire to make reparation, to make good the injury psychologically done to the mother and also to restore herself was at the bottom of the compelling urge to paint these portraits of her relatives. That of the old woman, on the threshold of death, seems to be the expression of the primary, sadistic desire to destroy. The daughter's wish to destroy her mother, to see her old, worn out, marred, is the cause of the need to represent her in full possession of her strength and beauty. By so doing the daughter can allay her own anxiety and can endeavour to restore her mother and make her new through the portrait.[12]

To the Lighthouse encodes the ambivalence of the girl child's relation to the mother, the need to destroy and then to make reparation. That Woolf herself harboured ambivalent and destructive feelings towards her mother we have already seen (Ch. 1): in *To the Lighthouse* she is permitted as author to commit matricide (in 'Time Passes'), while reparation has in fact already been made through the recreation of the mother in 'The Window'. On the element of reparation it is worth quoting Vanessa Bell, whose comments on the novel intersect interestingly with Klein's remarks quoted above:

> Anyhow it seemed to me in the first part of the book you have given a portrait of mother which is more like her to me than anything I could ever have conceived of as possible. It is almost painful to have her *so raised from the dead.* You have made one feel *the extraordinary beauty of her character*, which must be the most difficult thing in the world to do . . . You have given father too I think as clearly, but perhaps, I may be wrong, that isn't quite so difficult. There is more to catch hold of.[13] (my italics)

Klein's views on the psychic development of the girl child are illuminating in relation to *To the Lighthouse*, a novel in which sexual difference is so clearly a major theme and concern of the author. Given the date of publication, it is not surprising that there have been many Freudian analyses of this text: *To the Lighthouse*, as much as *Sons and Lovers,* has been considered an 'Oedipal' novel, exploring the passage through the Oedipal crisis of boy and girl children. While the novel as post-Freudian text can legitimately be interpreted in terms of classical Freudian analysis, it is important to register too the rather different emphasis to which a reading of *women* analysts (for example Klein and Horney) might lead us.

In a paper of 1945, Melanie Klein summarised the ways in which her view of the Oedipus complex differed from that of Freud.[14] The differences were mainly bound up with the significance attached to the penis, or phallus. Klein considers, briefly, that in the early development of children the mother plays the primary part, the child's relation to the penis, for example, being defined simply in terms of the mother's appropriation of something belonging to the father.

The mother, in other words, is seen as primary and active, the father as relatively passive, and the phallus is not the determining, all-important agent which it appears to be for Freud. Klein's lack of phallocentricity thus contrasts markedly with the emphasis in the analytic work of Freud. Her work opens up the possibility of a difference for feminist reading: too often feminist readings of texts such as *To the Lighthouse* replicate the phallocentricity of the Freudian version of the Oedipus complex.

James in *To the Lighthouse* identifies his mother (or his phantasy of his mother, his ideal mother) as the self-contained source of life and creativity. In a famous passage from 'The Window', the perceived impotence of his father is the exact model for James's feeling of impotence when his mother turns from him (an impotence recalled to memory years later on the trip to the lighthouse):

Mrs Ramsay, who had been sitting loosely, folding her son in her arm, braced herself, and, half turning, seemed to raise herself with an effort, and at once to pour erect into the air a rain of energy, a column of spray, looking at the same time animated and alive as if all her energies were being fused into force, burning and illuminating (quietly though she sat, taking up her stocking again), and into this delicious fecundity, this fountain and spray of life, the fatal sterility of the male plunged itself, like a beak of brass, barren and bare. He wanted sympathy ... It was sympathy he wanted, to be assured of his genius, first of all, and then to be taken within the circle of life, warmed and soothed, to have his senses restored to him, his barrenness made fertile, and all the rooms of the house made full of life.[15]

The reversal of conventional expectations in this passage (for example, it is *the man* who wishes his barrenness to be made fertile) confounds any simple reading of this passage in terms of the Freudian Oedipal moment, in which the boy responds to the father's threat of castration. While James does see his father as a rival for his mother's affection, he does not see his father as all-powerful, nor as capable of entirely rupturing the bond between his mother and himself. Later, too, his feelings of hostility to his father are qualified by protective feelings, for as Klein points out in her critique of Freud, 'in his good aspects the father is an indispensable source of strength', a model and guide who confirms the identity of the son. The son will identify with and therefore wish to preserve the father, as James does, thinking of his father in the following way on the shared journey to the lighthouse:

> There he had come to feel, quite often lately, when his father said something which surprised the others, were two pairs of footprints only; his own and his father's. They alone knew each other. (*TL*, p. 249)

The omnipotence of the father in the 'family romance' plot is also challenged in this text through the particular emphasis Woolf places on the mother–daughter relation. The text foregrounds Mrs Ramsay's relations with her eldest and youngest daughters, and with her surrogate daughter, Lily Briscoe. The Demeter/Persephone myth (a central cultural representation of the mother–daughter relation, and one with great resonance for Woolf) is explicitly invoked in connection with both Cam and Prue Ramsay. In the scene involving the boar's skull (which looks back to the image of the ram's skull in *Jacob's Room*), Mrs

Ramsay 'covers' the skull/male sexuality for her daughter while preserving it intact for James, and is thus linked with the mythical mother Demeter who is at once opposed to and necessarily complicit with patriarchal law. Like Demeter, Mrs Ramsay must accede to her daughter's 'fall' into sexuality: unlike Demeter, she foresees all that will happen, but still 'covers' this fall and presents it as a 'lovely' journey into a valley/garden of flowers:

> She quickly took her own shawl off and wound it round the skull, round and round and round, and then she came back to Cam and laid her head almost flat on the pillow beside Cam's and said how lovely it looked now . . . and Cam was repeating after her how it was like a mountain, a bird's nest, a garden . . . and Mrs Ramsay went on saying still more monotonously, and more rhythmically and more nonsensically, how she must shut her eyes and go to sleep and dream of mountains and valleys and stars falling and parrots and antelopes and gardens, and everything lovely, she said. (*TL*, pp. 154–5)

The reference is even more explicit in relation to Mrs Ramsay's eldest daughter, Prue. After her death in 'some illness connected with childbirth', Lily thinks of her retrospectively as Persephone, letting fall her basket of flowers in deference to Demeter/Mrs Ramsey's will:

> She let her flowers fall from her basket, scattered and tumbled them on to the grass and, reluctantly and hesitatingly, but without question or complaint – had she not the faculty of obedience to perfection? – went too. Down fields, across valleys, white, flower-strewn – that was how she would have

painted it ... They went, the three of them
together, Mrs Ramsay walking rather fast in front,
as if she expected to meet someone round the
corner. (*TL*, p. 271)

Mrs Ramsay is seen as complicit with a male-
dominated social order, especially from the point of
view of the adult Lily Briscoe, who deplores her
match-making activities. Yet this is not to say that the
strong mother–daughter bond suggested by the references to the Dememeter/Persephone myth is entirely
imaginary, or the product of fantasy, as Mary Jacobus
has suggested.[16] Jacobus, unwilling to move away
from the Lacanian view of this, sees the bond
between mother and daughter as existing only in
retrospective fantasy: if it exists, it exists in the
inaccessible pre-Oedipal world of the Lacanian
Imaginary, before the birth of subjectivity and
language. Melanie Klein, however, argues for a strong
identification with the mother *for both sexes* in earliest
childhood. Klein contends that this identification is
remembered and carried over into later life: she writes
of 'the far-reaching and lasting influence of every facet
of the relation to the mother'.[17] If Klein suggests that
the relationship is not fantasised, but real, Irigaray, as
we have seen, would go further and suggest that the
girl's early, pre-verbal relationship with the mother
creates a gender-specific 'inter-subjectivity' which
could form the basis for a subversion or alteration of
the existing symbolic order. Like *Mrs Dalloway*, *To the
Lighthouse* could be read as moving towards the
inscription of such an inter-subjectivity, through an
intimacy like that of 'waters poured into one jar' (*TL*,
p. 70)

The 'far-reaching' influence of the mother–daughter
relation is illustrated most clearly through the experi-

ence of Lily Briscoe. We are given no information in the text about Lily's biological mother, but Lily (connected with Elizabeth Dalloway through her enigmatic Chinese features) passionately identifies with Mrs Ramsay as a mother-figure, finding her immensely attractive. Lily's feelings are of powerful attachment to this woman with whom she wishes to merge and identify, in Part One of the novel at least:

> Could loving, as people called it, make her and Mrs Ramsay one? for it was not knowledge but unity that she desired, not inscriptions on tablets, nothing that could be written in any language known to men, but intimacy itself, which is knowledge, she had thought, leaning her head on Mrs Ramsay's knee. (*TL*, p. 70)

Lily wants to keep and to privilege the bond with the mother, rejecting the marriage plot which Mrs Ramsay herself constantly urges on her. Resisting the injunction to 'marry, marry', Lily 'breaks the sequence' (an activity which Woolf in *A Room of One's Own* linked with the need to recognise the truth that 'sometimes women do like women'). Wrenching the novel away from the marriage plot, Lily translates its terms of reference so that resolution and climax occur not through (hetero)sexual relations but through a woman's representation of another woman in art.

Lily's attachment to Mrs Ramsay is modified during the course of the text, so that the belief quoted above that 'intimacy ... is knowledge' is more tentatively expressed in the final section ('Who knows even at the moment of intimacy, This is knowledge?' asks Lily, p. 232). The change comes about, of course, because the relationship with Mrs Ramsay is interrupted by the 'cut' of death, which is experienced by

Lily as if she herself were implicated in it, as if she had felt the urge to destroy the mother which Melanie Klein posits as part of the girl's development. In the section of the novel 'Time Passes', the abandoned house represents the body of the dead mother, open to exploration by 'certain airs', just as Mrs Ramsay is open to Lily's exploration through memory in Part Three ('One wanted most some secret sense, fine as air, with which to steal through keyholes and surround her where she sat knitting', pp. 266–7). Seen as a corpse, the house/body is open to defilement, suggested through images of brutish sexuality:

> Listening (had there been anyone to listen) from the upper rooms of the empty house only gigantic chaos streaked with lightning could have been heard tumbling and tossing, as the winds and waves disported themselves . . . and mounted one on top of another, and lunged and plunged in the darkness or the daylight (for night and day, month and year ran shapelessly together) in idiot games, until it seemed as if the universe were battling and tumbling, in brute confusion and wanton lust aimlessly by itself. (*TL*, p. 183)

Images of miscegenation are also associated with the 'rotting', ruined house ('Let the wind blow; let the poppy seed itself and the carnation mate with the cabbage', p. 188). The retreat of the mother leaves the body and the primal scene to be viewed once again as horrific, as in *The Voyage Out*, in scenes far removed from the 'rosy' and positive review of the primal scene in Part One of the novel. The death of the mother is conflated, too, with the outbreak of war. The description of the decaying body/house is punctuated by references to the death and suffering caused by the war, as if to suggest the connection between militarism and a 'masculine' economy.

It is also as though the precarious sense of identity of the female (writing) subject is erased in this section of the novel, and to this extent 'Time Passes' moves towards the unstable discourse of madness. Throughout this section of the text, there is no 'character' to act as 'reflector', no subject to whom the perceptions of the narrative can be attributed. The text foregrounds this instability, with repeated use of the phrases 'as if' or 'it seemed', and the use of rhetorical questions. The lack of a subject to whom the discourse can be anchored is linked with a more general 'unravelling' in the text, a loss of confidence in the natural relations between the self and the external world. The 'natural' correspondences between self, word and world can no longer be relied on:

> That dream, then, of sharing, completing, finding in solitude on the beach an answer, was but a reflection in a mirror, and the mirror itself was but the surface glassiness which forms in quiescence when the nobler powers sleep beneath? Impatient, despairing yet loth to go (for beauty offers her lures, has her consolations), to pace the beach was impossible; contemplation was unendurable; the mirror was broken. (*TL*, pp. 182–3)

It is the death of the mother which brings about this crisis of representation, destroying any sure sense of connection between word and world, or signifier and signified. So this 'matricidal' central section of the novel might suggest that it is the problematic of access to a female voice and/or a female tradition (symbolised, in the novel, by Mrs Ramsay) which makes it so difficult for Lily Briscoe to paint. Throughout the first section of the novel Lily is shown self-consciously measuring herself against male expectations, and finding herself wanting. In isolation, like a child without a guiding mother, she struggles to defend the difference of her view:

> It was in that moment's flight between the picture and her canvas that the demons set on her who often brought her to the verge of tears *and made this passage from conception to work as dreadful as any down a dark passage to a child*. (*TL*, p. 28)

Having (metaphorically) destroyed the adored/feared mother in the person of Mrs Ramsay, Lily finds when she returns to the Ramsays' house after an absence of ten years that her projected painting has become more meaningless than ever, 'curves and arabesques flourishing round a centre of complete emptiness'.

Lily's ability to fill this empty space will be dependent on her establishing a particular relation with Mrs Ramsay as (dead) mother-figure. Again, this relationship may be illuminated by reference to Melanie Klein's view of mother–child relations. Particularly relevant to *To the Lighthouse* is Klein's linking of the (widespread) childhood experience of an 'infantile depressive position' with the adult experience of mourning. In a paper of 1940, 'Mourning and its Relation to Manic-Depressive States', Klein argued that:

> in mourning the subject goes through a modified and transitory manic-depressive state and overcomes it, thus repeating, though in different circumstances and with different manifestations, the processes which the child normally goes through in his early development.[18]

In *To the Lighthouse*, Lily, I would argue, goes through a double process whereby she works through infantile responses to the mother-figure *at one and the same time* as she, as an adult, mourns the lost mother. The parallel with Woolf's own experience in writing *To the Lighthouse* is obvious. Woolf herself drew attention to the ways in which she had followed the processes of analysis in writing the novel, tunnelling back into early childhood experiences ('I suppose I did for myself what psychoanalysts do for their patients', *MB*, p. 81). She also noted the element of mourning/ memorialising in the novel, writing in her diary:

(But while I try to write, I am making up 'To the Lighthouse' – the sea is to be heard all through it. I have an idea that I will invent a new name for my books to supplant 'novel'. A new — by Virginia Woolf. But what? Elegy?)[19]

To the Lighthouse thus provides the occasion for an intense meditation on the girl child's early relationship with her mother, and an exploration of the way in which that relationship carries through into and structures adult life and, perhaps, artistic creativity. It could then be argued that one of the most significant aspects of the novel is the way in which Lily gradually comes to separate out different aspects of the mother-figure, distinguishing between the real mother (what Klein would call the 'external' mother), the mother as an internal object, and the mother as a figure of femininity. Lily has to recognise that the real mother, who might be figured by Mrs Ramsay sitting on the beach peering absurdly over her spectacles, is dead and has gone away – but not out of vindictiveness, or a desire to harm, as the child imagines. The 'real' or external mother's absence is simply a fact, to be

accepted on the same level as Mr Ramsay's touchstone of reality, the table:

> 'Mrs Ramsay! Mrs Ramsay!' she cried, feeling the
> old horror come back – to want and want and not to
> have. Could she inflict that still? And then, quietly,
> as if she refrained, that too became part of ordinary
> experience, was on a level with the chair, with the
> table. (*TL*, p. 272)

The mother as an internal object, on the other hand,
has to be retained if the child is to maintain a
sufficiently strong ego: in this sense, *To the Lighthouse*
could be said to dramatise the (belated) internalisation of the mother as a good object by Lily Briscoe.
Klein explains this process as follows:

> The inner world consists of objects, first of all the
> mother, internalised in various aspects and
> emotional situations. The relationships between
> these internalised figures, and between them and
> the ego, tend to be experienced – when persecutory
> anxiety is dominant – as mainly hostile and
> dangerous; they are felt to be loving and good
> when the infant is gratified and happy feelings pre-
> vail.[20]

Klein further stresses that identification with a good
and life-giving internalised object is an 'impetus
towards creativeness'. She writes:

> We find in the analysis of our patients that the
> breast in its good aspect is the prototype of
> maternal goodness, inexhaustible patience and
> generosity, as well as of creativeness. It is these
> phantasies and instinctual needs that so enrich the

primal object that it remains the foundation for hope, trust, and belief in goodness.[21]

It could be argued that in the first section of *To the Lighthouse* Lily is in the position of a 'lost' daughter, lacking the firm identification with the mother which will release her creativity. She is persecuted by the male view that women 'can't paint, can't write', and also experiences anxiety about the mother/Mrs Ramsay's rapaciousness, even cruelty ('she was alarming, too, in her way, high-handed', *TL*, p. 65). Lily's internal and external worlds are thus split and fragmented, and she cannot see how to bring things into relation one with another. She explains her desire to do this *through* her painting:

> But now – he turned, with his glasses raised to the scientific examination of her canvas. The question being one of the relations of masses, of lights and shadows, which, to be honest, he had never considered before, he would like to have it explained – what then did she wish to make of it? And he indicated the scene before them. She looked. She could not show him what she wished to make of it. (*TL*, p. 73)

After the break of 'Time Passes', it could be argued, Lily becomes able to incorporate Mrs Ramsay and internalise her as a 'good object'. She is able to admit her identity with as well as difference from Mrs Ramsay during those moments of anguish which lead up to the hallucinatory reappearance of the mother-figure. In the last section of the novel, Lily finds a way out of the 'lost daughter' position which has characterised her life, and thus finds a means to 'mother', so to speak, and authorise her painting and herself. She discovers, in other words, that Klein's 'inexhaustible patience and generosity, as well as . . . creativeness' exist within herself, as well as in Mrs Ramsay.

Melanie Klein paid relatively little attention to potential differences between the girl and boy child's internalisation of good and bad (mother) objects. However, the emphasis of her work, with its focus on the pre-Oedipal period and on the early strength of attachment to the mother, has laid the basis for a particular school of thought among object-relations theorists in the United States. The work of Dorothy Dinnerstein and Nancy Chodorow has been particularly influential in its account of a gender-specific bond between mother and daughter. They argue that because they are mothered by someone of the same gender, girls develop more fluid or permeable ego boundaries than boys, and a sense of self that is continuous with others. There is, of course, a striking similarity between this account and Luce Irigaray's arguments for a specifically female subjectivity (or 'inter-subjectivity'), based on response to the other and a refusal of a position of mastery in relation to the other.[22] American object-relations theory, and French feminism, so widely different in other ways, come together in this notion of a specifically feminine subjectivity, stemming from the close early relation to the mother. The question which then arises is that of the extent to which Woolf subscribed to this view of a specifically feminine subjectivity (and creativity) in *To the Lighthouse*.

It could be argued that in this novel Woolf explores fully the seductive idea/ideal of a specifically feminine subjectivity. In particular, she pays close attention to that relation between self and other which is central to the arguments of the feminist theorists mentioned above. In *To the Lighthouse* we are, for example, shown

Mrs Ramsay engaged in the same kind of 'unselfing' which we have noticed earlier in Clarissa Dalloway. Mrs Ramsay is equally aware of the ways in which the self may be considered as dispersed or split, particularly through the felt disjunction between conscious and unconscious selves:

> One after another, she, Lily, Augustus Carmichael, must feel, our apparitions, the things you know us by, are simply childish. Beneath it is all dark, it is all spreading, it is unfathomably deep; but now and again we rise to the surface and that is what you see us by . . . Not as oneself did one find rest ever, in her experience (she accomplished here something dexterous with her needles), but as a wedge of darkness. Losing personality, one lost the fret, the hurry, the stir. (*TL*, pp. 85–6)

Just as Mrs Ramsay accomplishes 'something dexterous with her needles', so as this passage continues Woolf dexterously leads us to a paradox. To know the other, the self must be 'emptied' and the ego obliterated precisely in order that the ego, quiddity, selfhood *of the other* may be recognised, so that the other, in short, may be known as self:

> It was odd, she thought, how if one was alone, one leant to things, inanimate things; trees, streams, flowers; felt they expressed one; felt they became one; felt they knew one, in a sense were one; felt an irrational tenderness thus (she looked at that long steady light) as for oneself. (*TL*, p. 87)

The recognition of otherness implies both an act of projective identification whereby the other is 'selfed' and an act of separation whereby this pseudo-self is othered. It could be argued that in *To the Lighthouse*

Woolf suggests not only that this kind of recognition is most easily achieved in same-sex relationships, but also, perhaps, that it is more readily achieved by women. In a key passage during the *boeuf en daube* scene, for example, Mrs Ramsay is contrasted with Mr Carmichael, as they both contemplate a dish of fruit:

> Rose's arrangement of the grapes and pears, of the horny pink-lined shell, of the bananas, made her think of a trophy fetched from the bottom of the sea, of Neptune's banquet, of the bunch that hangs with vine leaves over the shoulder of Bacchus (in some picture), among the leopard skins and the torches lolloping red and gold ... Thus brought up suddenly into the light it seemed possessed of great size and depth, was like a world in which one could take one's staff and climb up hills, she thought, and go down into valleys, and to her pleasure (for it brought them into sympathy momentarily) she saw that Augustus too feasted his eyes on the same plate of fruit, plunged in, broke off a bloom there, a tassel, here, and returned, after feasting, to his hive. That was his way of looking, different from hers. But looking together united them. (*TL*, p. 131)

A difference in scale reflects the difference between Mrs Ramsay's depropriative and Mr Carmichael's appropriative approach to the fruit (which might figure either femininity or the origin of knowledge). To Mrs Ramsay the object of her gaze becomes 'a world' (and is, so to speak, 'selfed' as she correspondingly diminishes in size), while Mr Carmichael decentres and scatters that 'world', seizing on fragments which he 'breaks off' for his own consumption.

Woolf is explicit here about a difference of view

between Mrs Ramsay and Mr Carmichael, a difference of view which will be replicated at the close of the
novel as Lily Briscoe and Mr Carmichael gaze out to
sea side by side. In each case, Woolf registers a
difference while stressing complementarity – for 'looking together united them'. As this parallel would
suggest, in *To the Lighthouse* a gender-specific subjectivity is linked with a gender-specific approach to art.
In this novel the connexions between Mrs Ramsay's
creativity in life and Lily's creativity in art are
stressed. In an early passage, for example, Mrs
Ramsay is likened to a flower closing its petals in
'exquisite abandonment to exhaustion' after respond-
ing to and fertilising the 'fatal sterility' of the male
(*TL*, pp. 52–4). The vulval, flower metaphor suggests
female sexuality, positively viewed. Years later Lily
(whose 'flower' name also suggests female sexuality,
as well as purity) experiences exactly the same
exhaustion as she nears the completion of her painting
– she feels 'suddenly completely tired out', her mind
and body having been 'stretched . . . to the utmost'
(*TL*, p. 280). The metaphor of orgasm, the 'rapture of
successful creation', closely connects the two women:
it is as though Mrs Ramsay's sexual creativity
provides an origin and a sponsoring analogy for Lily's
particular kind of (female) artistic creativity. This
relates to the point made earlier in connection with
Mrs Dalloway about the need to define, or imagine, a
'feminine' creativity in a period of a 'sexualisation' of
aesthetics.

If it is the case that Woolf subscribes to the notion of
a specifically 'feminine' subjectivity/creativity in *To
the Lighthouse*, it would follow that Lily's painting could
be interpreted as representing, in some sense,
'feminine' painting. The significance of Lily's painting, and in particular of the final 'line' in its centre,

has been much debated by feminist critics. Gayatri
Spivak, for example, has read the line as cancelling the
vacillation of 'Time Passes', figuring the (imaginary)
wholeness of a beauty which is 'self-identical', for
which Lily longs.[23] Mary Jacobus, on the other hand,
has suggested that the line figures the imaginary
plenitude of the phallic mother. Alternatively Jacobus
suggests that the line might be that which fixes Lily
and the book, 'placing both in a stabilising, specular
relation to artist and author', or that it could be the
line of minimal difference that makes possible the
process which Kristeva calls abjection.[24] It has also
been argued that the line establishes a relationship
between the 'polarities' of masculine and feminine
which would otherwise remain mutually exclusive,
unrelated.[25] None of these readings can be discounted,
but a further view can be added. If we examine the
passage where Lily begins the painting, we can see
Lily's self-inscription/the inscription of Mrs Ramsay
as the making of a feminine mark, as the inscription of
a femininity which unsettles the phallogocentric
symbolic order. As Lily marks her canvas, Woolf
describes the strokes of her painting in terms which
directly recall Mrs Ramsay's orgasmic experience as
she sits looking at the lighthouse beam: both Lily's
painting and Mrs Ramsay's *jouissance* are, it could be
argued, rooted in a female sexuality and identity
which is not defined in relation to the phallus. Lily
begins her painting in this way:

> With a curious physical sensation, as if she were
> urged forward and at the same time must hold
> herself back, she made her first quick decisive
> stroke. The brush descended. It flickered brown
> over the white canvas; it left a running mark. A
> second time she did it – a third time. And so

pausing and so flickering, she attained a dancing
rhythmical movement, as if the pauses were one
part of the rhythm and the strokes another, and all
were related; and so lightly and swiftly pausing,
striking, she scored her canvas with brown running
nervous lines which had no sooner settled there
than they enclosed (she felt it looming out at her) a
space. Down in the hollow of one wave she saw the
next wave towering higher and higher above her.
(*TL*, pp. 213–14)

Subsequently, as the space and mass of the canvas
loom before her, we are told that Lily dips into the
blues and umbers 'as if some juice necessary for the
lubrication of her faculties were spontaneously
squirted'. Her mind moves 'like a fountain spurting
over that glaring, hideously difficult white space,
while she modelled it with greens and blues' (*TL*,
pp. 215–16).

The metaphor of female orgasm and female sexual
pleasure might lie behind this passage, as it more
obviously underlies the description of Mrs Ramsay's
ecstasy as she looks at the lighthouse beam and her
creation of a 'fountain' of reassurance for her husband.
It could be that Woolf uses sexual metaphors in her
description of Lily painting in order to link feminine
sexual and artistic creativity and to validate the latter
through the former. In this passage Woolf presents the
mark of painting/articulation as driven by an autonomous feminine desire which finds expression
through the rhythmical modelling (shaping, sculpting)
of 'white space' into the waves/arabesques of female-
defined form. In such a reading, the phallus neither
conditions nor constrains the 'painful but exciting
ecstasy' which Lily feels, and the line which she places
at the centre and at the end of her painting could be

seen as a feminine marking or scoring of the canvas, centring the difference of her (feminine) view.

This reading can be supported by the text: however, the problem with it is one common to all discussions of a specifically 'feminine' inscription, which by definition can work only on the margins of the existing symbolic order. This 'femininity' can be felt only as rhythm, echo, suggestion: its existence in a text (or painting) cannot be precisely demonstrated. A further difficulty is, I think, more significant for our interpretation of *To the Lighthouse* as a whole. It can be argued that the writing of Virginia Woolf works towards the introduction into the symbolic order of that which has been repressed within it, especially the feminine/the body. What happens then, however, is only too familiar: in an attempt to articulate 'the new', the feminist writer/artist ends up with something which is uncannily like the old. For in whatever way we define the feminine as different, we risk ending up with a category which exists only in a negative relation to the existing order, and which can also be viewed as both restrictive and divisive. I think that Woolf felt this, and that we can see a wariness about 'the feminine' beginning to surface in *To the Lighthouse* in Lily's meditations on Mrs Ramsay not as 'real' or introjected mother, but as a figure representative of femininity.

In this respect, Woolf's text begins to move from an articulation of the feminine as ideal to an examination of the feminine as it has been culturally constructed. In the final part of the book, for example, we are made sharply aware of the way in which Mr Ramsay's masculinity and Mrs Ramsay's femininity existed (in the past) as a binary opposition in which each term was constantly struggling for mastery. The couple were locked in a sterile opposition in which neither could escape or transcend their gender stereotype. Towards the end of the novel, Lily considers further the limitations of the feminine role as Mrs Ramsay conceived it:

> Mrs Ramsay has faded and gone, she thought. We can over-ride her wishes, improve away her limited, old-fashioned ideas. She recedes further and further from us . . . Life has changed completely. *At that all her being, even her beauty, became for a moment, dusty and out of date.* For a moment Lily, standing there, with the sun hot on her back, summing up the Rayleys, triumphed over Mrs Ramsay, who would never know how Paul went to coffee-houses and had a mistress; how he sat on the ground and Minta handed him his tools; how she stood here painting, had never married, not even William Bankes. (*TL*, p. 236)

Lily's awareness here that 'masculinity' and 'femininity' are culturally constructed roles which are subject to change puts pressure on the notion of a transcendent feminine ideal. In the light of Lily's awareness, it is significant that even Mrs Ramsay's *beauty* begins to fade. At moments such as this, I'd argue, the 'romance' of femininity has gone from the text, and this is what Lily recognises at the very end of the novel. She sees that conceptions of femininity *are* visions, which must continually be revised and re-negotiated. In future texts Lily's vision ('I have had my vision', p. 281) will be revised and qualified, as Woolf begins to explore different ways of contesting the cultural construction of gender difference.

4 Imaginary Lives: *Orlando* and *A Room of One's Own*

Orlando

It is possible to detect elements of guilt over trans-
positions from Woolf's (mother's) life to the text of *To
the Lighthouse*, and we can, I think, find evidence of a
similar compunction in relation to *Orlando*. *Orlando* is a
mock-biography of Vita Sackville-West, whom Woolf
first met in 1922, and with whom she fell in love.
Nigel Nicholson writes that her relationship with
Vita was 'the deepest relationship which Virginia ever
had outside her family'. Both Nicholson and Quentin
Bell are inclined to play down the sexual element in
the relationship, but Sherron E. Knopp argues that:

> . . . the letters between Virginia and Vita, published
> in 1978 and 1984 respectively, reveal an attachment
> that lasted in its physical expression not just the
> 'few months, a year perhaps' that Nicholson first
> speculated but at least two years beyond that and
> probably more, and it continued in emotional
> intensity until Virginia's death in March 1941.[1]

Orlando is in a very real sense a *public* celebration of the
woman Woolf loved. It is dedicated to Vita, and the
first edition contained several photographs of Vita
posing as Orlando. There were dangers, of course, in
making such a public declaration of 'Sapphic' love,

and in identifying Orlando so unequivocally with Vita Sackville-West. Woolf was aware of such dangers, but also showed a certain recklessness over the potentially scandalous nature of her book. When she first writes to Vita asking her permission to go ahead with *Orlando*, she seems already seduced by her own subject, caught up in erotic linguistic play:

> But listen; suppose Orlando turns out to be Vita; and its all about you and the *lusts* of your flesh and the *lure* of your mind (heart you have none, who go gallivanting down the lanes with Campbell) – suppose there's the kind of *shimmer* of reality which sometimes attaches to my people, as the *lustre* on an *oyster* shell . . . suppose, I say, that Sibyl next October says 'There's Virginia gone and written a book about Vita' . . . Shall you mind? Say yes, or No.[2] (my italics)

Yet despite this carelessness over the publicity of her 'love letter' to Vita (as Nigel Nicholson calls *Orlando*), there is a compensating thread of imagery in the novel which suggests ambivalence, and perhaps guilt, over the textualisation of a living woman. In several passages in the novel Woolf evokes a sense of trance or stasis which is at first puzzling, unless we read these frozen, static scenes as metaphors for the process of embalming which the novel itself undertakes. Early in the novel, for example, we have the following passage:

> Shoals of eels lay motionless in a trance, but whether their state was one of death or merely of suspended animation which the warmth would revive puzzled the philosophers. Near London Bridge, where the river had frozen to a depth of

some twenty fathoms, a wrecked wherry boat was plainly visible, lying on the bed of the river where it had sunk last autumn, overladen with apples. The old bumboat woman, who was carrying her fruit to market on the Surrey side, sat there in her plaids and farthingales with her lap full of apples, for all the world as if she were about to serve a customer, though a certain blueness about the lips hinted the truth.[3]

The old bumboat woman is like Vita (whose name, of course, means 'life'): fixed, frozen, pinned down by Woolf's prose. To textualise a person is to fix them, to appropriate them, in a manner which might well trouble Woolf. Yet beneath this level of concern over appropriation, there is a deeper sense of unease evidenced in the text which might relate to Kristeva's notion of 'abjection'. To write a person into a text is to translate them into a medium which is neither living nor dead and thus perhaps to transgress or unsettle the fixed boundary between life and death and evoke the experience of abjection. Woolf's awareness of such a disturbing or transgressive potential of writing is suggested in a later passage in *Orlando* on Sir Thomas Browne (whose texts deal, of course, in mortality):

Like an incantation rising from all parts of the room . . . rolled the divine melody of those words which, lest they should outstare this page, we will leave where they lie entombed, not dead, embalmed rather, so fresh is their colour, so sound their breathing (*O*, p. 78)

Despite this sombre element in the text, all Woolf's comments on the production of *Orlando* emphasise the enjoyment which she had out of writing it. She

planned it as 'an escapade; the spirit to be satiric, the
structure wild', and subsequently described it as 'all a
joke; and yet gay and quick reading I think; a writer's
holiday'.[4] Recently, it has been argued that Woolf's
representation of the novel as a 'joke' has prevented
readers and critics from seeing its deeper themes – and
yet *Orlando* has been the object of serious critical
attention for some years. Most notably, it has been
considered in relation to the theme of androgyny by
such critics as Elaine Showalter, Sandra Gilbert and
Gillian Beer.[5] More recently, lesbian feminist critics
such as Sherron E. Knopp have read the text as a
'celebration' of Vita's Sapphic nature, written 'with
an insider's knowledge'. I want, however, to approach
the text first through its connexion with *To the
Lighthouse*.

It has long been recognised that the passage in
Chapter 2 of the novel, in which Woolf describes the
passing of the seasons and the changes wrought by
time, is a parody of the 'Time Passes' section of *To the
Lighthouse* (the part of the book she was most anxious
about when it was published). It could also be argued,
however, that in other sections of *Orlando* Woolf
satirises elements of the earlier novel: elements,
perhaps, over which she felt vulnerable. In particular,
it could be argued that Woolf satirises aspects of Mrs
Ramsay through the figure of Orlando as a woman.
Mrs Ramsay is not, of course, a fixed character, but
her textual experiences reflect, as has been suggested
in Chapter 3, an idealised view of the 'feminine'
principle. Yet in *Orlando*, Mrs Ramsay's very words
('ecstasy', 'rapture') are echoed and parodied, and her
conception of the role of the woman is by implication
mocked. We might compare the following passage, for
example, with many of the descriptions of Mrs
Ramsay in *To the Lighthouse*:

Which is the greater ecstasy? The man's or the
woman's? And are they not perhaps the same? No,
she thought, this is the most delicious (thanking the
Captain but refusing), to refuse, and see him frown.
Well, she would, if he wished it, have the very
thinnest, smallest shiver in the world. This was the
most delicious of all, to yield and see him smile.
'For nothing', she thought, regaining her couch on
deck, and continuing the argument, 'is more
heavenly than to resist and to yield; to yield and to
resist. Surely it throws the spirit into such a rapture
as nothing else can.' (*O*, p. 149)

The very juxtaposition of food and emotional susten-
ance is reminiscent of the *boeuf en daube* scene in *To the
Lighthouse*. Subsequently, Orlando reflects on the
distinction between the external (man's) world and
woman's interior life in terms which again echo *To the
Lighthouse*. Women, freed from martial ambition and
the love of power can, she thinks, 'more fully enjoy the
most exalted raptures known to the human spirit'.
The comic exaggeration of tone here distances us from
an emotion whose contingent and constructed nature
is made abundantly clear. Orlando begins to construct
these responses not because she has become a woman
in the biological sense, but because of the restricted
opportunities offered to women under patriarchy. As
she reflects, 'women are not (judging from my own
short experience of the sex) obedient, chaste, scented,
and exquisitely apparelled by nature' (*O*, p. 150).
Woolf's understanding of the constructed nature of
femininity here looks forward to the analysis of gender
in *The Years*. Woolf through Orlando (interestingly in
relation to her earlier work) also expresses reserva-
tions about the idealisation of one's own sex:

'Praise God that I'm a woman!' she cried, and was about to run into the extreme folly – than which none is more distressing in woman or man either – of being proud of her sex. (*O*, p. 154)

If femininity is constructed, what, then, are the relations between biological sex, psychological gender, and identity? In *Orlando*, Woolf begins to explore the disjunctions between these, where she had earlier assumed continuity. In the famous discussion of clothing (often related to Woolf's supposed advocacy of androgyny), Woolf/the narrator asserts unequivocally that Orlando's *identity* is not changed by the change of biological sex:

But in every other respect, Orlando remained precisely as he had been. The change of sex, though it altered their future, did nothing whatever to alter their identity. (*O*, p. 133)

'Her' psychological gender does, however, appear to change. Just as Orlando, after becoming a woman, has to wear a (restricting) skirt and petticoats, so she must alter her behaviour in order to conform to the expectations which society has of those marked as 'women'. So:

. . . all seems to hint that what was said a short time ago about there being no change in Orlando the man and Orlando the woman, was ceasing to be altogether true. She was becoming a little more modest, as woman are, of her brains, and a little more vain, as women are, of her person . . . Orlando curtseyed; she complied; she flattered the good man's humours. (*O*, p. 180)

Woolf's suggestion, then, accords with current feminist thinking: gender is constructed and is not necessarily linked either to sex or to identity. However, Woolf then appears to contradict herself. Having argued for the artificial construction of gender, she then seems to suggest that there is a 'natural' link between clothes and what lies beneath:

> The difference between the sexes is, happily, one of great profundity. Clothes are but a symbol of something hid deep beneath. It was a change in Orlando herself that dictated her choice of a woman's dress and of a woman's sex. (*O*, pp. 180–1)

Here, the suggestion seems to be that gender is not arbitrary but essential, the expression of a difference which is fundamental ('one of great profundity' 'hid deep beneath'). What are we to make of this apparent contradiction? The metaphors of surface and depth offer a clue. What lies 'beneath' sex, gender and identity is, in Freudian terms, the 'psychic bisexuality' of the earliest phase of human life. Orlando's 'choice' of a different sex (and then concomitant gender/ identity) might, then, signal a return *in fantasy* to this early stage of psychic bisexuality, or vacillation. This would accord with Woolf's own suggestion in *Orlando* that:

> Different though the sexes are, they intermix. In every human being a vacillation from one sex to the other takes place, and often it is only the clothes that keep the male or female likeness, while underneath the sex is the very opposite of what it is above. (*O*, p. 181)

Emphasising the importance of fantasy, one way of reading the text would be to connect it with psychic bisexuality, and indeed *Orlando* can be read as an allegory of the development of femininity which has several points of convergence with Freud's account of such development. In *Orlando*, it could thus be argued, Woolf gives us not only an account of historical development from the Elizabethan period to 'the present', but also, metaphorically, an account of the development of an individual feminine subject.

In Freudian thought, earliest childhood is marked by a condition of bisexuality, as desire shifts across 'masculine' and 'feminine' objects. Freud writes that 'freedom to range equally over male and female objects' is a distinguishing feature of early life.[6] Lacan also sees 'psychical bisexuality' as one of the most important of Freud's concepts, and connects this with the precarious nature of all subject-identification. In an essay published in 1986, Francette Pacteau relates such psychic bisexuality to the 'impossible' ideal of androgyny, which she sees as representing a 'dual sexual identity'. She argues that while the androgyne does not exist in the real, as a figure of fantasy s/he is attached to archaic memories of early childhood. Androgyny belongs to the domain of the imaginary, where desire is unobstructed; gender identity to that of the symbolic, the Law. The androgynous-looking figure presents us with an impossibility, that of the erasure of the very difference which constitutes us as subjects. In the encounter with the androgyne, the adult is able to shift positions, oscillating between the masculine and the feminine, and this 'recalls' the undifferentiated sexuality of the pre-Oedipal period:

> Our identity is constructed – in similarities and differences – in identification with whomever we

grow up with. Subsequently the everyday encounter with the other reminds us incessantly of this identity. When the other is not identifiable, my own position wavers. The consequent psychic oscillation would allow me, so to speak, to regain my other half, to reform the ideal image lost and found in the mirror.[7]

In this account, the androgyne (as a figure of fantasy) offers the possibility of a fantasised re-enactment of earlier pleasures, a return to the state of wholeness which pre-exists, so to speak, the arbitrary 'splitting' of the Oedipal moment, when as subjects we line up, for ever, on one side or other of the gender divide. At the same time, the androgyne embodies the threat of dissolution: as Pacteau puts it, 'from dual sexual identity to non-sexual identity, in effect non-identity, there might be only one step.' Hence, perhaps, the powerful hold which the figure of the androgyne has on the imagination, compounded of a mixture of desire and dread.

Woolf wrote 'How extraordinarily unwilled by me but potent in its own right, by the way, *Orlando* was!'[8] As Gillian Beer has noted,[9] the first part of *Orlando* constitutes the most powerful section of the text. Perhaps this is because in it both Orlando and Sasha are presented in terms of a 'dual sexuality' which troubles the reader and makes her/his position 'waver'. Sasha, for example, is first presented in the following terms:

The person, whatever the name or sex, was about middle height, very slenderly fashioned, and dressed entirely in oyster-coloured velvet, trimmed with some unfamiliar greenish-coloured fur. But these details were obscured by the extraordinary seductiveness which issued from the whole person. Images, metaphors of the most extreme and extravagant twined and twisted in his mind. He called her a melon, a pineapple, an olive tree, an emerald, and a fox in the snow ... But the skater came closer. Legs, hands, carriage, were a boy's, but no boy ever had a mouth like that; no boy had those breasts; no boy had eyes which looked as if they had been fished from the bottom of the sea. (*O*, pp. 36–7)

'Obscurity' and distance enable the fantasy of androgyny to operate. Sasha's 'extraordinary seductiveness' depends precisely on the 'wholeness' of (her) person marked with both 'male' and 'female' biological and psychosexual attributes. (The category of the 'psychosexual' is helpful here because it denotes the 'grey' area in between physiological sexual difference and the sociological category of gender. Freud discusses psychosexual difference in terms of a contrast between *activity* and *passivity*. We tend, of course, to associate activity with the masculine, passivity with the feminine, but in the pre-Oedipal, according to Freud, passive and active instinctual aims alternate in both male and female subjects.) Sasha, then, is to Orlando both 'a melon' (suggesting, perhaps, the female breasts, and also stasis or passivity) *and* 'a fox in the snow' (suggestive of the phallus and of activity).

Sasha and Orlando do not, then represent an androgynous ideal in the sense in which some earlier commentators have understood it. They are not to be taken as figuring a synthesis of 'masculine' and 'feminine' characteristics in a single harmonious person, for such balance would imply the *denial* of undifferentiated sexuality. Rather, their image allows for the possibility (for the spectator and/or each other) of an oscillation between 'masculine' and 'feminine' positions (or 'vacillation', in Woolf's word).

The 'indeterminacy of sex' in the first part of *Orlando* could, then, be linked with the psychic bisexuality of the pre-Oedipal period, and Orlando's change into a woman could be seen as analogous to the little girl's acquisition of gender in the Freudian account of female development. The difficulties which Orlando experiences in her progress through the eighteenth, nineteenth and twentieth centuries could be linked with the difficulties which the little girl has, in Freud's account, in adapting to her gendered role. Freud maintains that the girl has greater difficulty than the boy in passing through the Oedipus complex. When the little boy, threatened by the possibility of castration, must repress his early desire for his mother, he is able to do this by identification with the father-figure. Possessing the phallus, he can look forward to the day when he too will possess a woman like/in place of the mother. The little girl, on the other hand, must redirect her early desire for her mother, and orient herself towards a male rather than a female love-object. With the recognition of sexual difference and of castration, Freud suggests, the little girl begins to repudiate her (similarly castrated) mother. She turns to the father in the hope of deriving from him first a penis, and subsequently a baby to stand in place of the unattainable penis. The mechanism by which the desire for the biological father is then displaced and deferred remains unclear in Freud's account.

Freud recognises (some of) the difficulties attendant upon the acquisition of an appropriately 'feminine' identity, and hypothesises that there are three lines of development open to the girl when she becomes aware of the fact of castration. She can retreat from sexuality altogether, feeling her inadequacy, 'frightened by the comparison with boys'. Alternatively, she can cling to her threatened masculinity, fantasising the possession of a penis. This leads to what Freud calls a 'masculinity complex' and, possibly, a homosexual choice of object. The third path – to 'normal femininity' – Freud describes as 'very circuitous':

> Only if her development follows the third, very circuitous, path does she reach the final normal female attitude, in which she takes her father as her object and so finds her way to the feminine form of the Oedipus complex. Thus in women the Oedipus complex is the end-result of a fairly lengthy development.[10]

Adrienne Rich and others have objected to Freud's account of female development, arguing, in particular, that there is no compelling reason why the little girl should ever direct her search for love away from her own sex. Rich writes:

> If women are the earliest sources of emotional caring and physical nurture for both female and male children, it would seem logical, from a feminist perspective at least, to pose the following questions: whether the search for love and tenderness in both sexes does not originally lead toward women; *why in fact women would ever redirect that search*; why species survival, the means of impregnation, and emotional/erotic relationships should ever have become so rigidly identified with each other.[11]

Rich's questions form part of her wider argument against 'compulsory heterosexuality', and it could be objected that in contesting this form of oppression (which *is* an oppression) Rich is led into an over-valuing of her own sex and of same-sex relationships. If this is the case, it is an over-valuation of which Woolf is also on occasion guilty, perhaps for similar strategic reasons. (It has been argued earlier that same-sex relations, inextricably involved with the memory of the first relationship with the mother, form a crucial imaginative ideal for Woolf.)

In *Orlando*, the moment of castration – Orlando's recognition of the fact that she is a woman – is followed not by a repudiation of the feminine, but by an intensification of feminine identification. Orlando thus follows the trajectory which Rich sketches, and which, it could be argued, *is already implicit in* Freud's troubled account of female development. After she has 'become' a woman, Orlando's primary object of love remains a woman, and her feelings towards Sasha are not weakened but intensified. For Orlando:

> . . . if the consciousness of being of the same sex had any effect at all, it was to quicken and deepen those feelings which she had as a man. For now a thousand hints and mysteries became plain to her that were then dark. Now, the obscurity, which divides the sexes and lets linger innumerable impurities in its gloom, was removed, and if there is anything in what the poet says about truth and beauty, this affection gained in beauty what it lost in falsity. At last, she cried, she knew Sasha as she was . . . (*O*, pp. 154–5)

Same-sex relationships are celebrated: the (idealising) suggestion is that they offer a greater possibility for communication. 'Falsity' will mar relationships in which there is an imbalance of power, as there is in heterosexual relationships within patriarchy. This

love/relationship between Orlando and Sasha may
also be a *reprise* of the earliest relation with the mother.
Woolf described her own relationship with Vita
Sackville-West in terms which suggest a connection
for her between lesbian love and a return to the
mother:

> In brain and insight she is not as highly organised
> as I am. But then she is aware of this and so
> lavishes on me the maternal protection which, for
> some reason, is what I have always most wished
> from everyone.[12]

Woolf's treatment of same-sex relationships is
complex, and varies through her fiction. Here there is
a strong sense of an affirmation of 'feminine' identity
through the doubling/mirroring of same-sex relations
(as there is in Irigaray's considerations of 'female
homosexuality'). What the 'feminine' might signify
remains problematic: on the one hand, as we have
seen, Woolf stresses the constructed nature of 'femininity' in *Orlando* (and hence the possibility of its
changing); on the other, she continues to celebrate its
value, for example in a letter to Vanessa Bell written
at more or less the same time as *Orlando*. While
recognising the need for change, Woolf continues to
value some aspects of (constructed) femininity highly.
Like Cixous, she celebrates the fluidity and fertility
which she connects with 'the feminine'. So she writes
to her sister, using Cixousian images of water and
gardens:

> You will never succumb to the charms of any of
> your sex – What an arid garden the world must be
> to you! What avenues of stone pavements and iron
> railings! Greatly though I respect the male mind,

and adore Duncan (but, thank God, he's herm-
aphrodite, androgynous, like all great artists) I
cannot see that they have a glowworm's worth of
charm about them – The scenery of the world takes
no lustre from their presence. They add of course
immensely to its dignity and safety: but when it
comes to a little excitement – ![13]

Orlando's progress thus seems to confirm what Freud
intuited and Rich forcefully argues for, that is, the
difficulty for the female child of redirecting her love
from the mother to the father, and the continuity
between her early, exclusive love for the mother and
same-sex ties in later life. However, Orlando is finally
forced to accommodate herself to 'normal' femininity:
here again her experience seems to parallel that of the
little girl in Freud's analysis. Woolf shows very clearly
the social pressures which drive Orlando to take up a
female reproductive role within patriarchy. These
pressures reach a critical point in the Victorian period
(also the period under scrutiny in *The Years*). It is in
this period that the family becomes the crucial
organising unit in society: hence the importance and
sanctity of 'the home – which had become extremely
important' (*O*, p. 218). Woolf also notes the corres-
ponding emphasis on 'compulsory heterosexuality' in
the Victorian period, an emphasis which, Orlando
thinks, is not 'natural':

At the same time, she began to notice a new habit
among the town people . . . Couples trudged and
plodded in the middle of the road indissolubly
linked together. The woman's right hand was
invariably passed through the man's left and her
fingers were firmly gripped by his . . . Orlando
could only suppose that some new discovery had
been made about the race; that they were somehow

stuck together, couple after couple, but who had
made it, and when, she could not guess. It did not
seem to be Nature. She looked at the doves and the
rabbits and the elk-hounds and she could not see
that Nature had changed her ways or mended
them, since the time of Elizabeth at least. (*O*,
p. 231)

In this passage, Woolf has recourse to the category of
'Nature' in order to expose the 'unnatural' quality of
social organisation. She anticipates the insights of
Foucault and of Adrienne Rich in underlining the way
in which as contemporary subjects we must find our
identity through the *constructed* categories of sex and
gender. As Rich argues, species survival, the means of
impregnation, and emotional/erotic relationships
have become 'rigidly identified with each other', so
that, as Woolf describes it, 'couple after couple' are
'stuck together' in the institution of compulsory
heterosexuality which ensures the reproduction of
patriarchal society.

Orlando is worked on by what Woolf calls the 'spirit
of the age', which inclines her, 'step by step' to submit
to the new discovery of coupledom. The change in
Orlando is not brought about by the discovery of a
'natural' love/desire for a man, overriding the earlier
preference for her own sex. Instead, Woolf suggests
that it is a process of insidious weakening and
belittlement which brings Orlando to the point of
seeking the protection of a man. As the nineteenth
century progresses, Orlando is brought to perceive
herself as physically weak and in need of protection
against the onslaughts of rapacious male sexuality:

So she strayed out into the park alone, faltering at
first and apprehensive lest there might be poachers

or gamekeepers or even errand-boys to marvel that
a great lady should walk alone.

At every step she glanced nervously lest some
male form should be hiding behind a furze bush . . .
(*O*, p. 236)

The contrast between the impetuous young Orlando
and this timid creature suggests that this weakness is
not 'natural' but constructed. In Freudian terms, we
might say that in Victorian society activity is assigned
to men, passivity to women, to such an extent that in
Orlando's case she comes to see death as the only way
out of her position of helplessness. Going out onto the
moor in *Wuthering Heights* fashion, she breaks her ankle
(rather like Catherine Linton, whose 'fall' can be
linked with the onset of puberty), and falls into a
passive trance:

'I have found my mate,' she murmured. 'It is the
moor. I am nature's bride,' she whispered, giving
herself in rapture to the cold embraces of the grass
as she lay folded in her cloak in the hollow by the
pool. 'Here will I lie.' (A feather fell upon her
brow.) (*O*, p. 237)

It is at this point that Orlando is 'rescued' by
Marmaduke Bonthrop Shelmerdine. She marries and
has a son, thus extending her family tree. She also
completes her poem *The Oak Tree*, from within the safe
haven of a marriage which (just about) conforms to
convention. There are clear parallels here not only
with Vita Sackville-West, but with Woolf herself.

In *Orlando*, then, Woolf gives an account of female
development which tallies in many respects with the
Freudian account. The text sympathetically treats
psychic bisexuality/androgyny and the same-sex

attachments of Orlando, but some scepticism is shown over Orlando's later accommodation to woman's role in patriarchy. This is reflected in a passage towards the end of the novel in which Woolf offers a compressed version of some of the key scenes in *To the Lighthouse*. The gender-inflected, oppositional images through which Mrs Ramsay justifies her marriage are quite emptied of significance in this parodic repetition, which offers a satirical rewriting of the lyrical ending of *To the Lighthouse*:

> She looked into the darkness. There was her husband's brig, rising to the top of the wave! Up, it went, and up and up. The white arch of a thousand deaths rose before it. Oh rash, oh ridiculous man, always sailing, so uselessly, round Cape Horn in the teeth of a gale! But the brig was through the arch and out on the other side; it was safe at last!
>
> 'Ecstasy!' she cried, 'ecstasy!' And then the wind sank, the waters grew calm; and she saw the waves rippling peacefully in the moonlight. (*O*, p. 312)

A Room of One's Own

In *A Room of One's Own*, Woolf reverses the trajectory of *Orlando*. In this text, instead of moving from psychic bisexuality to gendered identity, the reader is invited first to consider the construction of gender hierarchies, then to explore the possibility of their subversion. In the first two chapters of *A Room of One's Own* the narrator (identified as a textual requirement rather than a living being: ' "I" is only a convenient term for somebody who has no real being'[14]) reproduces for the reader the experience of being constructed as a gendered subject. When the text begins, the narrator is sunk in reverie. The dead metaphor is given back life as Woolf evokes the experience, the flux of thought:

> Thought – to call it by a prouder name than it deserved – had let its line down into the stream. It swayed, minute after minute, hither and thither among the reflections and the weeds, letting the water lift it and sink it . . . (*R*, p. 6)

The narrator is startled out of this state by the famous appearance of the Beadle – 'a man's figure rose to intercept me' – and is chased off the turf. It takes her a moment to move out of her (ungendered) reverie and to (re)construct herself as a feminine subject:

> Instantly a man's figure rose to intercept me. Nor did I at first understand that the gesticulations of a curious-looking object, in a cut-away coat and evening shirt, were aimed at me. His face expressed horror and indignation. Instinct rather than reason came to my help: he was a Beadle; I was a woman.

For 'instinct', we can read 'trained instinct': certainly there is no basis *in reason* for the hierarchical structure of gender whereby the masculine is invariably construed as dominant. In *A Room of One's Own*, Woolf underlines the arbitrary nature of gender difference through such means as the apparently whimsical reference to a cat with no tail ('It is strange what a difference a tail makes – you know the sort of things one says . . . '), and explores the ways in which male dominance is expressed and secured institutionally. The narrator is physically excluded from an Oxbridge library, and consequently feels disinclined to enter King's College Chapel: she is an outsider, barred from certain kinds of knowledge/power. When, in search of 'the truth' about women she enters the more democratic portals of the British Museum, it is only to find 'W' endlessly defined by men in terms of inferiority. Woolf's spoof index makes the point:

South Sea Islanders, age of puberty among,
Attractiveness of,
Offered as sacrifice to,
Small size of brain of,
Profounder sub-consciousness of,
Less hair on the body of,
Mental, moral and physical inferiority of,
Love of children of . . . (*R*, p. 37)

It is at this stage in the text that Woolf develops the 'looking-glass theory' of gender difference. Men insist on women's inferiority, she argues, in order to confirm their own superiority. Like all colonised groups, those marked as women must be 'othered' if existing power-relations are to be maintained:

Hence the enormous importance to a patriarch who has to conquer, who has to rule, of feeling that great numbers of people, half the human race indeed, are by nature inferior to himself. It must indeed be one of the chief sources of his power . . . Women have served all these centuries as looking-glasses possessing the magic and delicious power of reflecting the figure of man at twice its natural size. (*R*, p. 45)

The implication is that women can only operate within the constraints of patriarchy as surfaces with no depth, mirroring that 'confidence in oneself' which men have created precisely by denying the alterity of women.

Woolf thus reads gender as a Derridean binary opposition, in which one term is (falsely) assumed to be derivative from and secondary to the other. One response which women can make to this oppositional structure is to try and reverse its terms, from man/woman to woman/man. At one point in *A Room of One's Own*, it seems that this is the path which the narrator is going to take, literally and figuratively. After lunching in an Oxbridge college, she makes her way to 'Fernham', a women's college which can only be found 'if you take the right turning' (*R*, p. 17). When she arrives at this women's enclave, she finds that 'something odd' is at work, and the season suddenly undergoes a transformation, from autumn to spring:

> The gardens of Fernham lay before me in the spring twilight, wild and open, and in the long grass, sprinkled and carelessly flung, were daffodils and bluebells, not orderly perhaps at the best of times, and now wind-blown and waving as they tugged at their roots. The windows of the building, curved like ships' windows among generous waves of red brick, changed from lemon to silver under the flight of the quick spring clouds ... and then on the terrace, as if popping out to breathe the air, to glance at the garden, came a bent figure, formidable yet humble, with her great forehead and her shabby dress – could it be the famous scholar, could it be J— H— herself? (*R*, p. 21)

As we have seen, Woolf often uses the metaphor of the garden to suggest the particular quality of women's relationships with women, and the metaphor of the flower, particularly the rose, is frequently used to figure female sexuality and creativity. Here, we note too that the garden is 'wild and open', not orderly but 'wind-blown'. This wild and generative garden might, then, recall the Cixousian celebration of the feminine principle, and of feminine sexuality, which is evident in other texts by Woolf, for example *Mrs Dalloway* and *To the Lighthouse*. The sea metaphor ('waves of red brick') used by Cixous to figure women's *jouissance* is here, as are the colours of lemon and silver which thread through Mrs Ramsay's autoerotic, orgasmic reverie in *To the Lighthouse* ('it silvered the rough waves ... it rolled in waves of pure lemon', p. 89). The garden of 'Fernham' (the name suggests fertility, with perhaps an echo of Jane Eyre's 'Ferndean') can thus be seen as a metaphor which incorporates those characteristics which Woolf had earlier connected with 'the feminine' as an ideal.

The fact that Woolf changes the season to spring to introduce the garden suggests other resonances. This spring garden calls up the image of Persephone, and thus also of Demeter, who is also figured in the text in the appearance of 'J. H.' The initials stand for Jane Harrison, a scholar whose work on pre-classical Greek goddesses was well known to Woolf, especially her work on the myth of the Mother and the Maiden, which evolved into the Demeter–Persephone myth.[15] This passage in *A Room of One's Own* thus connects female sexuality or *jouissance* not only with the love of women rather than men but also with the 'originary love story' with the mother. Woolf introduces her description of a women's college by calling attention to the primary bond between women which is authorised in our culture (the mother–daughter bond) and then merges the figures of mother, teacher, and female lover in the person of 'J.H.', much as she did in the 'Sapphist' story 'Slater's Pins Have No Points', written in 1927.

Woolf turns back, however, from the path of celebration of the feminine in *A Room of One's Own*. Rather than reversing the terms of the opposition man/woman by privileging the feminine, she works towards a destabilising of this opposition. In Chapters 3 and 4 of *A Room of One's Own*, for example, Woolf is often said to rewrite feminine literary history in order to create an alternative 'female tradition', anticipating the work of later critics such as Sandra Gilbert and Susan Gubar, for example. However, such an assertion must be qualified by the recognition that Woolf continually stresses the contingency of all value in *A Room of One's Own*, rather than stressing the primacy of any particular value-system. She highlights, too, the impossibility of ever 'measuring' values according to an 'objective' standard:

> Is it better to be a coal-heaver or a nursemaid; is the charwoman who has brought up eight children of less value to the world than the barrister who has made a hundred thousand pounds? It is useless to ask such questions; for nobody can answer them. Not only do the comparative values of charwomen and lawyers rise and fall from decade to decade, but we have no rods with which to measure them even as they are at the moment. (*R*, p. 51)

The very method of *A Room of One's Own*, with its shifting viewpoints and sudden juxtapositions, encourages us to see 'truth' as varying and unstable, and value as dependent on point of view. The text, then, does not argue for the primacy of women's values, for this would be simply to replace one dominant perspective with another. Rather, Woolf calls for a multiplication of different perspectives, in literature as in life. Woolf wants, in Cixous's phrase, to 'stir up differences', to 'cheer them on'. She endorses difference as non-exclusive and as multiple, and seeks to go beyond binary oppositions such as that between the two sexes:

It would be a thousand pities if women wrote like men, or lived like men, or looked like men, for if two sexes are quite inadequate, considering the vastness and variety of the world, how should we manage with one only? Ought not education to bring out and fortify the differences rather than the similarities? For we have too much likeness as it is, and if an explorer should come back and bring word of other sexes looking through the branches of other trees at other skies, nothing would be of greater service to humanity. (*R*, p. 114)

One method of destabilising the opposition between the sexes might be precisely by introducing the theme of Sapphism, not in order to privilege same-sex relations above other relationships/identities, but in order to explore the possibility of 'different' relationships which cut across those fixed alignments of sex/gender/identity which are both assumed and imposed as a norm in our society. (Sapphism was Woolf's own term for this element in *A Room of One's Own*: she wrote in her diary of her fear that she would be 'attacked for a feminist and hinted at for a Sapphist' when the book was published.[16])

Woolf's Sapphism can in fact be read on several levels in this text. On the one hand, it can be read as a kind of challenge to the Oedipal plot as outlined/prescribed by Freud. As we have seen, Freud describes female homosexuality as one possible route which is open to the girl after the realisation of castration. This line:

leads her to cling with defiant self-assertiveness to her threatened masculinity. To an incredibly late age she clings to the hope of getting a penis some time. That hope becomes her life's aim; and the phantasy of being a man in spite of everything often persists as a formative factor over long periods. This 'masculinity complex' in women can also result in a manifest homosexual choice of object.[17]

Freud can only understand female homosexuality in terms of male heterosexuality: for him the aims and objects of these two positions are identical. In other words, he is unable to imagine *a woman* desiring another woman. It was not until the 1970s that Freud's view of female homosexuality was challenged by various psychoanalytically-informed feminist discussions of female sexuality. The work of Dorothy Dinnerstein, Nancy Chodorow and, of course, Adrienne Rich emphasised the homoerotic mother–daughter bond of the pre-Oedipal phase as a crucial determinant of female sexual difference. Woolf's writing, as we have seen, returns obsessively to this bond, which is in *A Room of One's Own* inextricably entwined with the motif of Sapphism, particularly through the use of Jane Harrison (lesbian and archaeologist of the pre-classical Greek goddesses) as a Demeter-figure.

Woolf's Sapphism can thus be read as an attempt to move away from Freud's three lines of female development towards a fourth dimension, although her work cannot of course be read as a direct response to Freud. In such a reading, her Sapphism (which might be defined as a 'lyrical lesbianism', the figure of Sappho conveniently uniting the two elements) might be seen as a response to and a rejection of the institution of compulsory heterosexuality, which in both its social and psychic manifestations rests on subordination to male power and a disavowal of the mother. We might thus read Woolf's Sapphism as John Fletcher suggests we read contemporary lesbianism:

> lesbianism can be seen as a restorative strategy which seeks to *repair* the losses, denigrations, thwartings that a patriarchal culture inflicts on the girl in her primary relation to the mother.[18]

On, as it were, a deeper level, we could read Woolf's lesbianism, especially its textual inscription, in the light of Luce Irigaray's ideal of 'female homosexuality'. This female homosexuality must be distinguished from the 'hommosexuality' which Irigaray punningly suggests is constitutive of the patriarchal social order. According to Irigaray, patriarchy operates around the male-as-subject: at the moment, women can only occupy an object position. Irigaray suggests that the current subject-predicate structure of language 'presupposes woman as universal predicate'.[19] This is why, for Irigaray, the question of the symbolisation of the feminine/the mother in language is so crucial. For the little girl, her first other (the mother) is perceived as an object *with whom she must identify*, because she is of the same sex.[20] So women perceive *themselves* as an object, and woman's weak, 'object' position is endlessly perpetuated. In order for a woman to enter language as a subject, she must be able, as Margaret Whitford puts it, 'to make a female identification with her mother that does not objectify her'. Woman, therefore, must be symbolised *as woman*, as distinct from as mother/object. So Margaret Whitford writes:

> A woman's first address to the other, her first 'you' [*tu*] should be to another woman, but for this to be

possible the mother and woman *must* be symbolic-
ally differentiated. Hence the need for a female
homosexual economy, and for a genealogy on the
mother's side.[21]

For Irigaray, the need is to symbolise, shape and
represent a 'female homosexual economy' which
would give woman a place in which 'her' difference
could be articulated and recognised. Women's love for
each other, as actual or spiritual mothers and
daughters or sisters, offers the *locus* for the emergence
of such a new subjectivity and syntax. Irigarary
writes:

> We lack, we women with a sex of our own kind
> [nous sexuées selon notre genre], a God in which to
> share, a word/language [verbe] to share and to
> become. Defined as the often obscure, not to say
> hidden, mother-substance of the word/language
> [verbe] of men, we lack our *subject*, our *noun*, our *verb*
> [verbe], our *predicates*: our elementary sentence, our
> basic rhythm, our morphological identity, our
> generic incarnation, our genealogy.[22]

Irigaray's 'female homosexuality' is thus intimately
bound up with her utopian vision of a future beyond
patriarchy.

Woolf's Sapphism can thus be read in relatively
straightforward terms as bound up with a 'return' to
the mother (and here the psychoanalytic views of Rich
and Chodorow might be invoked); or it can be
interpreted more abstractly (in its textual manifestation) as moving towards the symbolisation of a
difference which has not yet been articulated in
western patriarchal culture. The second view is
supported, perhaps, by Woolf's suggestion in *A Room*

of One's Own that if a woman were really to express herself:

> the resources of the English language would be much put to the stretch, and whole flights of words would need to wing their way *illegitimately* into existence. (*R*, p. 113, my italics)

Alternatively, the lesbian element in *A Room of One's Own* can be interpreted in a more direct political sense, as it has been most notably by Jane Marcus. Marcus focuses particularly on Woolf's allusions in *A Room of One's Own* to the contemporary trial for obscenity of Radclyffe Hall's *The Well of Loneliness*. Woolf alludes in the published text first to Sir Charles Biron (presiding magistrate in the case), then to Sir Archibald Bodkin (director of public prosecutions): in both instances, the allusions occur in the context of an affirmation of 'liking women'. So Marcus concludes that:

> In her deliberate marriage of *A Room of One's Own* to *The Well of Loneliness*, Woolf's narrative strategy of intertextuality with a banned and 'obscene' lesbian novel is a political effort to keep lesbian texts in print, if only by allusion. She wins her 'room' only to share it.[23]

Marcus's argument is supported by the fact that in the draft for *A Room of One's Own*, *Women and Fiction*,[24] Woolf is more explicit in her references both to the Radclyffe Hall trial and to erotic relations between women.

In *A Room of One's Own*, Woolf thus begins to explore the relations between feminist and lesbian perspectives in radical ways, anticipating more recent attempts to theorise the links between the two perspectives.[25] 'Sapphism', it can thus be argued, operates in this text to 'break the sequence' of both phallocentrism and compulsory heterosexuality, problematising their (re)production in physical, psychical and textual terms.

The deconstruction of gender oppositions in *A Room of One's Own* can also be traced through Woolf's famous discussion of androgyny in the final chapter. This is the part of the text which has provoked more commentary than any other. The narrator, prompted by the agreeable sight of a couple getting into a taxi, begins to speculate about the androgynous mind of the artist, contrasting the 'androgynous' Coleridge and Shakespeare with the exclusively 'virile' Galsworthy and Kipling:

> And I went on amateurishly to sketch a plan of the soul so that in each of us two powers preside, one male, one female; and in the man's brain the man predominates over the woman, and in the woman's brain the woman predominates over the man. (*R*, p. 128)

One of the most influential reactions to Woolf's 'androgyny' has been that of Elaine Showalter in *A Literature of Their Own* (1977). Showalter contends that Woolf's vision of androgyny is 'inhuman', and that it represents an escape from, rather than an exploration of 'femaleness or maleness'.[26] Two more recent accounts, however, point the way to a rather different reading. In her discussion of *A Room of One's Own*, Sue Roe suggests that the most significant moment in the last chapter is that when a single leaf is seen to fall from a tree:

The fall of the leaf seems to symbolise a new order of things, but not only that: it seems suggestive of an entirely new mood. A feeling of peace and containment prevails; the pause feels pregnant . . .[27]

This insight is suggestive, and draws our attention to the different levels at work simultaneously in this text. Below, so to speak, the level of argument, Woolf seems here to touch the unconscious, which is, surely, the 'current' which brings together the images of the young man, the young woman and the taxi. Rachel Bowlby's reading[28] would seem to support such an interpretation: she emphasises the fact that in the 'androgyny' passage, we do not have unmediated access to the 'girl' and 'young man'. Nor do we have such access to the 'man-womanly' couple who are presented in the following famous passage:

Some marriage of opposites has to be consummated. The whole of the mind must lie wide open if we are to get the sense that the writer is communicating his experience with perfect fullness. There must be freedom and there must be peace. Not a wheel must grate, not a light glimmer. The curtains must be close drawn. The writer, I thought, once his experience is over, must lie back and let his mind celebrate its nuptials in darkness. (*R*, p. 136)

What we have instead is a triangular structure, in which the presence of the narrator-as-voyeur complicates the presentation of androgyny. In other words, what is presented in these scenes is not androgyny, but, crucially, a *fantasy* of androgyny. It could be argued, then, that the *fantasy* of androgyny in *A Room of One's Own* is related to the fantasy of the first

part of *Orlando*, and that both refer back to the
unconscious and, ultimately, to the 'psychic bisexuality' of the earliest stage of existence. The terms
of Woolf's description of Coleridge's androgynous
mind in *A Room of One's Own* are certainly suggestive of
the undivided state of the pre-Oedipal:

> He meant, perhaps, that the androgynous mind is
> resonant and porous; that it transmits emotion
> *without impediment*; that it is naturally creative,
> incandescent and *undivided*. (*R*, p. 128, my italics)

The 'androgynous vision' for which Woolf is celebrated
might, then, be anything but androgynous in that it
involves, as in *Orlando*, a *disavowal* rather than a
balancing of gender differences.

It was suggested in Chapter 1 that the passage just
quoted, in which Woolf describes the 'marriage of
opposites', was a version of the 'primal scene', and
that one of its most significant features was its
encoding of the feminine role in consummation/
creativity. While the representation of the feminine
position is an important element, it is also true that
one of the most remarkable aspects of this scene is its
'mobility', the term which Jean Laplanche and J. B
Pontalis use to denote the fluid positionality of 'primal
fantasies'. Laplanche and Pontalis argue that primal
fantasies combine a fixity of terms with fluidity in their
narrative combination and staging, so that in such
fantasies, subject positioning is the effect of a desiring
movement through the terms and images of the
narrative. This well describes the oscillation, or
mobility, of this scene.

If *A Room of One's Own* works on many levels, one
which should not, finally, be overlooked is that of the
'untold' story which shadows the text. As Jane

Marcus and other critics have noted, two important figures haunt about the margins of the text: Mary Hamilton and Judith Shakespeare. While Judith Shakespeare is almost entirely Woolf's invention, Mary Hamilton comes from the Scots ballad of the 'Four Maries'. She sings the ballad, as one of Mary Queen of Scots' four maids-in-waiting, who is about to be hanged for murdering her illegitimate child. While Woolf mentions each of Mary Queen of Scots' other maids by name (Mary Beton, Mary Seton and Mary Carmichael) Mary Hamilton is omitted: the effect of the omission is, paradoxically, to identify her with the most important 'character' in *A Room of One's Own*, the narrator. The narrator also identifies passionately with Judith Shakespeare ('who shall measure the heat and violence of the poet's heart when caught and tangled in a woman's body?', she asks). The narrator is thus closely linked with two women who commit infanticide, while, on the other hand, an apparently serene and unproblematic equation between writing and giving birth is insisted on throughout the text. What is the reader to make of these apparent contradictions?

It could be argued that in deploying the metaphor of birth, Woolf is here working through, or against, a limit in writing itself. It is as though in this text writing is always edging up to a moment of birth which it can neither convey nor embody (as Woolf cannot tell the story of Mary Hamilton, and Judith Shakespeare cannot be born). In using the double infanticide/birth metaphor, is Woolf acknowledging the fact that writing cannot 'be' birth: it cannot embody that plenitude? *The Waves* explores in more detail the complex relations between writing and this (imaginary) plenitude, and between writing and death.

5 Generation(s) in *The Waves* and *The Years*

The Waves

In *The Waves*, Woolf returns to that primal scene of writing which plays its part in the structure of so many of her novels – *The Voyage Out*, *Jacob's Room*, and *To the Lighthouse*, for example. This scene, we remember, surfaces in 'A Sketch of the Past' in Woolf's evocation of the 'most important' of her early memories:

> It is of lying half asleep, half awake, in bed in the nursery at St Ives. It is of hearing the waves breaking, one, two, one, two, and sending a splash of water over the beach; and then breaking, one, two, one, two, behind a yellow blind. It is of hearing the blind draw its little acorn across the floor as the wind blew the blind out. It is of lying and hearing this splash and seeing this light, and feeling, it is almost impossible that I should be here; of feeling the purest ecstasy I can conceive. (*MB*, p. 73)

A version of this scene clearly forms the 'base' of *The Waves*, manifesting itself as the framing scene or (back)ground which supports and enfolds the whole text. The first interlude of the novel closely echoes (or rather anticipates) the description just quoted:

> The surface of the sea slowly became transparent and lay rippling and sparkling until the dark stripes

were almost rubbed out. Slowly the arm that held
the lamp raised it higher and then higher until a
broad flame became visible; an arc of fire burnt on
the rim of the horizon, and all round it the sea
blazed gold.

The light struck upon the trees in the garden,
making one leaf transparent and then another. One
bird chirped high up; there was a pause; another
chirped lower down. The sun sharpened the walls
of the house, and rested like the tip of a fan upon a
white blind and made a blue finger-print of shadow
under the leaf by the bedroom window. The blind
stirred slightly, but all within was dim and un-
substantial. The birds sang their blank melody
outside.[1]

Although this frame-scene changes in the novel as we
move from dawn to dusk and from spring to winter, it
is interesting that we start with dawn and a borderline
state. It is as though Woolf comes back again here to
the origins of self and writing, which are for her (as
was suggested in Chapter 1) conterminous if not
identical. In returning obsessively to this space
between land and sea, light and dark, night and day,
Woolf uncovers, as it were, the place in which writing
begins. In an excellent discussion of *The Waves*, Daniel
Ferrer makes a similar point, arguing that we can see
'the very space of writing' emerging in the following
lines which appear halfway through Woolf's first
outline for the novel:

Between the sun & the churchyard was a strip of
lawn; on this they could walk, as a shipman walks
his deck.[2]

The borderline scene which haunts Woolf (appearing,
also, for example, in *To the Lighthouse*, as Mrs Ramsay,

Lily, Mr Bankes and Mr Ramsey gaze out to sea) could be said, like that 'strip of lawn', to figure the space between the sun and the churchyard, between life and death, into which writing inserts itself.

Yet despite the abstract and figurative quality of writing (its 'deathly' aspect), Woolf attempts in *The Waves* to strain against this quality by broaching the 'issue' of the physical origins of the body. Knowledge of physical origin in the maternal body is, of course, something which many texts seek to repress. Freud describes in *The Interpretation of Dreams* the way in which knowledge of this origin may be screened and only obliquely represented in our dreams:

> In some dreams of landscapes or other localities emphasis is laid in the dream itself on a convinced feeling of having been there once before . . . These places are invariably the genitals of the dreamer's mother; there is indeed no other place about which one can assert with such conviction that one has been there once before.[3]

It could be argued that such knowledge surfaces in a similarly oblique way in many literary texts. In *The Waves*, indeed, Woolf herself censored the representations of bodily origin which appeared in the first drafts of the novel. She may have felt that these passages were too rudely transgressive, breaking cultural taboos. They show very clearly her fascination with maternal origins, and the connection between this theme and her recurrent use of the metaphor of the waves. This, for example, is one of three descriptions of birthing mothers which occur in the first pages of the first draft:

Many mothers, & before them
many mothers, & again many mothers, have groaned, & fallen
~~back, while the child crowed~~. Like one wave, ~~& then~~ succeeding
another. Wave after wave, endlessly sinking & falling as far as the eye can
stretch. And all these waves have been the prostrate forms of
mothers, in their ~~flowing~~ nightgowns, with the tumbled sheets about
them holding up, with a groan, as they sink back into the sea,
~~infin innumerable children~~.[4]

Here, the rhythmical repetition and the use of words
and phrases such as 'endlessly' and 'as far as the eye
can stretch' suggest a vanishing point of origin, an
origin which cannot be seized or penetrated. (The
phallic metaphor may not be entirely beside the point
here: Irigaray describes man's 'phallic' sexuality as an
attempt to 'penetrate' the mystery of the stomach from
which he came.) Neither sex can penetrate this
mystery, nor appropriate a relation to origin, but what
is significant is Woolf's admission here of the maternal
body which is conventionally elided. Woolf's sense of
the maternal body, if not as origin, as that which most
vividly *represents* origin to us, clearly makes its way
through into the imagery of the finished text of *The
Waves*. The rhythm of the waves which Woolf wanted
'to be heard all through' the novel thus suggests
maternal labour as well as female orgasm. Indeed, it
could be argued that in *The Waves* Woolf moves from
the rhythms of copulation/orgasm (so important
structurally in *Mrs Dalloway* and *To the Lighthouse*) to
the rhythms of labour as structuring, generating and
sponsoring her text. It is also significant that the body
of a woman is woven in with the descriptions of the

waves in the framing interludes. The woman's arms, her brows, her 'wide-opened' eyes are almost indistinguishable from the movement of the waves: it is as though the rhythmical pulsing of her body literally supports the text.

When Woolf first thought of writing *The Waves*, she speculated about the possibility of writing 'some semimystic very profound life of a woman', and she referred to the 'mystic' quality of the text on other occasions. This 'mystic' quality might be connected with the sense of *déjà vu* mentioned by Freud in the passage quoted above. The sense of mystery, even of the uncanny, which frequently marks the text may stem from Woolf's (re)presentation in it of the familiar/tabooed maternal body. Freud also writes in *The Interpretation of Dreams* of the 'uncanny' life before birth, and of the prevalence in adult life of fantasies of birth and of intra-uterine life. Perhaps not surprisingly, the metaphors of *The Waves* encode a complex preoccupation with birth and with intra-uterine life. For example, the famous episode in which Rhoda gazes at a puddle which she is unable to cross has been interpreted in Lacanian terms as connected with a failure to develop a unitary sense of self.[5] In this interpretation, the coherence of the mirror-image is said to mock the sense of dissolution of Rhoda as alienated subject. However, it could be argued that the scene also figures a return to the womb, in a complex reworking of key motifs:

> I came to the puddle. I could not cross it. Identity failed me. We are nothing, I said, and fell. I was blown like a feather, I was wafted down tunnels. Then very gingerly, I pushed my foot across. I laid my hand against a brick wall. I returned very painfully, drawing myself back into my body over

the grey, cadaverous space of the puddle. This is life then to which I am committed. (*W*, p. 50)

Freud maintains that, in fantasy, birth may be figured though a reversal and experienced as *entering* water.[6] Here, Rhoda's 'birth' is figured as the fall into the puddle/the womb and her agonising return down the birth canal (of tunnels and brick walls) is, for her, a metaphorical death (the return to a life to which she is, in Woolf's ambiguous phrase, 'committed'). Similarly, when Rhoda has a pre-vision of her own death, it is evoked through the metaphor of entering the waves, as though it too were a birth:

> Rippling small, rippling grey, innumerable waves spread beneath us. I touch nothing. I see nothing. We may sink and settle on the waves. The sea will drum in my ears. The white petals will be darkened with sea water. They will float for a moment and then sink. Rolling me over the waves will shoulder me under. Everything falls in a tremendous shower, dissolving me. (*W*, p. 171)

Suicide becomes a 'birth' into death, underlining the ambiguity which surrounds the birth metaphor for Woolf. It is as though in *The Waves* Woolf has moved beyond the fantasy of the maternal body as a wholly *secure* point of origin (although, as we have seen, Woolf seldom presents the maternal body without some equivocation). In *The Waves*, while she continues to invoke the maternal body as an emblem of female (pro)creative power, thus emphasising its positive aspects, she also explores its negative and potentially malign (symbolic) qualities. This shift coincides with the movement away from orgasm and towards birth as the dominant trope and organising metaphor of the text. In *The Waves*, Woolf focuses less on *jouissance* and female sexuality, and more on that aspect of women's creativity which implies its opposite. Birth is an 'origin' of which the 'supplement', to borrow Derrida's term, is death. In *The Waves* Woolf comes as near as is possible to the textual revelation of death.

In *The Interpretation of Dreams*, Freud writes in a footnote that:

> The act of birth is the first experience of anxiety, and thus the source and prototype of the affect of anxiety.[7]

This observation points to the possibility of a slightly different interpretation of the text's central trope of birth. Freud's remark suggests that birth can be seen as a kind of falling away from a primordial state of wholeness, and thus that the origin of being/ meaning could be located in the trauma of birth. In a modern (re)formulation of Freud, Elizabeth Bronfen has suggested that the *omphalos* or navel might operate as the sign of primary, non-gendered castration: the implication here is that the scene of birth might replace the scene of castration as a dominant metaphor for the origin of meaning.[8] Lacan, of course, contends that subjectivity, and therefore meaning, cannot be constituted until the child passes through the Oedipal crisis, at which point the phallus becomes the 'primary signifier' of all that we can never have, as subjects divided both from others and ourselves. Woolf's text, however, might be seen as presenting the mother's birthing body, rather than the phallus, as the *sign* of the crack of origin. In the opening interlude of the text, for example, as many commentators have noted, Woolf offers an allegory of 'the birth of self-consciousness'. However, the metaphor of birth is *unselfconsciously* used by such critics who fail to notice Woolf's explicit linking of the 'birth' of meaning not with the apprehension of sexual difference (as in Lacanian thought), but with the primary split from the mother. For example, in the famous opening interlude of *The Waves* Woolf presents the 'separation' between sea and sky – the creation of distinction, of meaning – via a metaphor which violently recalls the separation of the child's body from the amniotic fluid and maternal blood:

> Then she raised her lamp higher and the air seemed to become *fibrous* and *to tear away from the green surface* flickering and *flaming in red and yellow fibres* like the smoky fire that roars from a bonfire. (*W*, p.3)

Whichever way one interprets it, in *The Waves* birth figures as something of a scandal. In representing the crack or split of origin, it may suggest a 'fall' from that primary, ideal state of self-sufficiency which underpins many myths of origin. But, importantly, the fall from the mystic limit of the body of the mother also prefigures the ultimate scandal of death. It is as though in *The Waves* Woolf penetrates behind the screen of the *jouissant* mother-figure of earlier texts (as represented by Mrs Ramsay, for example) to a scene of origin which holds terror because it also opens onto death. It could be argued that contemplation of origin necessarily reminds us of our materiality and hence of mortality. Hence, perhaps, the fear of/disgust with the scene of birth which is so marked in the first drafts of the novel. The (re)production of animate life is viewed with horror by the 'hooded figure' who narrates the first draft of *The Waves*:

— To a sardonic eye—*& perhaps there was *(if there)*

an eye in the hooded figure at the table — nothing

could have been more ridiculous & base than ~~these~~ the

worm like, ~~eel~~ like. half conscious yet blindly impulsive

& violent actions of these little bald ~~brats~~ *animals*. And

soon the beach was covered with their markings.

Soon they were staggering across the sand. & leaving foot prints.

the toe of one touching the heel of another all across

~~what had been before a white, an immaculate~~

~~the~~ *&* blank ~~sheet~~.

Here we can also trace nostalgia for the 'blank sheet' of the 'immaculate' mother who, perhaps, screens off death in Woolf's earlier texts.

The way in which death is implicated in birth is underscored in many passages in *The Waves*, for example in the second 'interlude' as Woolf describes the opening of buds into flowers:

> As the light increased a bud here and there split asunder and shook out flowers, green veined and quivering, as if the effort of opening had set them rocking, and pealing a faint carillon as they beat their frail clappers against their white walls. (*W*, p. 21)

At the very moment of opening the flowers set in motion the faintest chiming, like that of church bells, suggestive of mortality. A very similar metaphor is used by Katherine Mansfield, in a letter to Middleton Murry first published in 1928. The intertextuality between *The Waves* and Mansfield's 'At the Bay' will be considered later in this chapter, but it is worth noting at this point the way in which both writers 'see' death in the moment of a flower's active unfolding. Mansfield writes to Murry:

> In a way it's a tragic knowledge: it's as though, even while we live again, we face death. But *through Life*: that's the point. We see death in life as we see death in a flower that is fresh unfolded.[10]

Rather similarly in *The Waves*, Susan, who, Gillian Beer has argued, comes to embody (or incarnate) the maternal principle, intimately connects birth and death in the following passage:

> I am fenced in, planted here like one of my own trees. I say, 'My son', I say, 'My daughter', and even the ironmonger looking up from his counter strewn with nails, paint and wire-fencing respects the shabby car at the door with its butterfly nets, pads and bee-hives . . . I also make wreaths of white flowers, twisting silver-leaved plants among them for the dead, attaching my card with sorrow for the dead shepherd, with sympathy for the wife of the dead carter; and sit by the beds of dying women, who murmur their last terrors, who clutch my hand; frequenting rooms intolerable except to one born as I was and early acquainted with the farmyard and the dung-heap . . . (*W*, 158–9)

It is as though in becoming 'gravid' with *The Waves*, Woolf 'sees' death: indeed, as Daniel Ferrer has pointed out, in sketching her first idea for the book, she also anticipated her own death, her '*fin*' (meaning 'end' in French of course) in a 'waste of waters'. Woolf noted the origin of the novel in a vision of 'a fin passing far out'.[11] The phrase recurs in the text of *The Waves*, and when she finished the novel Woolf recorded that:

> I have netted that fin in the waste of water which appeared to me over the marshes of my window at Rodmell when I was coming to an end of *To the Lighthouse*.[12]

The discussion up to this point might seem to suggest that Woolf's preoccupation with death in this novel should be seen negatively. However, although disgust/fear of death is registered in the text, particularly in passages like that in the third interlude, which describes a rotting and 'purulent' world beneath the flower beds, it could also be argued that in *The Waves* Woolf moves towards an 'incorporation' of death which can be viewed rather differently.

Hélène Cixous has written about the need to reach out to death rather than to repress it, and has suggested that a writing which 'touches' life will also 'touch' death. She writes, for example, of Clarice Lispector's *The Hour of the Star*:

> The text deals with the relationship between living and writing. The latter nevertheless always interrupts something of the flow of life. Writing is triggered by a kind of vibration, a kind of bodily music, but, even though it traverses the body, it begins in the head. Another, more violent kind of writing goes further, deeper, as a musical writing, signed, bearing a proper name, but detached from the author, in the direction of death.[13]

We can, I think, find such a 'deeper', 'musical' kind of writing in *The Waves*, particularly in the long section

towards the close of the novel in which Bernard
explores a 'world without a self'. Here Bernard
undergoes a kind of death: the 'self' dissolves, and
with it the hierarchies and oppositions which structure
conscious life. The familiar hierarchy between subject
and object is undone as the subject loses the appetite
for appropriation:

> Now it was done with. I had no more appetites to
> glut; no more stings in me with which to poison
> people; no more sharp teeth and clutching hands or
> desire to feel the pear and the grape and the sun
> beating down from the orchard wall. (*W*, p. 238)

In this state, Bernard describes himself as 'a dead
man'. It is as though for Woolf (as for Cixous) death
can represent a supreme loss of self-consciousness
which does not necessarily destroy the subject. Rather,
the necessary violence of death allows the admission of
the other, of that which lies outside the self:

> I saw the fields rolling in waves of colour beneath
> me, but now with this difference; I saw but was not
> seen. I walked unshadowed; I came unheralded.
> From me had dropped the old cloak, the old
> response; the hollowed hand that beats back
> sounds. Thin as a ghost, leaving no trace where I
> trod, perceiving merely, I walked alone in a new
> world, never trodden; brushing new flowers, unable
> to speak save in a child's words of one syllable;
> without shelter from phrases. (*W*, p. 239)

In this state, 'perceiving merely', Bernard has recourse
to what Woolf calls a few pages further on 'a little
language such as lovers use'. In death as in love, the
other is not subordinated to the self, nor to the system

of signs ('proper' language) which secures the dominance of the subject. The world which Bernard sees is
singular, unique, untranslatable:

> I need . . . words of one syllable such as children
> speak when they come into the room and find their
> mother sewing and pick up some scrap of bright
> wool, a feather, or a shred of chintz. (*W*, p. 246)

This is not quite, perhaps, the world of the radically
alien Kristevan semiotic, but it is one in which a
primary language is sought which will enable the
object to exist independently of the subject's needs
and desires. A 'new' relation between subject and
object requires a new language. That this is also a
relation dating back to childhood and the early
relation with the mother, is suggested as Woolf/
Bernard describes the inadequacy of conventional
language:

> But how describe the world seen without a self?
> There are no words. Blue, red – even they distract,
> even they hide with thickness instead of letting the
> light through. How describe or say anything in
> articulate words again? – save that it fades, save
> that it undergoes a gradual transformation,
> becomes, even in the course of one short walk,
> habitual – this scene also. (*W*, p. 239)

It is notable that Bernard here goes back to (or,
strictly speaking, anticipates) Woolf's first memory,
invoking the primary colours of the mother's dress
mentioned in 'A Sketch of the Past' ('purple and red
and blue', *MB*, p. 72). This would suggest that, as I
have argued earlier, the period of close early relation
with the mother is not necessarily one without

language (*pace* Lacan), but one in which (a) language
operates differently. The language which Bernard
desires is one which will catch the light of that which is
not the self, and it is a language, or an articulation of
meaning, which, the text suggests, has been experienced before. It is this language/interrelation of early
childhood which provides one 'base' for Woolf's
aesthetic project in *The Waves*.

It is important, of course, that it is Bernard who
carries the burden of speech in this last section of the
novel. Does Woolf's use here of a male narrator
suggest that writing and/or the pursuit of a 'world
without a self' is not gendered in this text? This
question is related to another which is frequently
posed about this novel: are we to view the six
characters represented in it either as separate individuals or as aspects of one person? Woolf herself
seems to imply both. The characters are quite firmly
distinguished from each other by the continual repetition of iconic phrases and images – Louis, for example,
detached from 'the boasting boys', connected with the
past and the women by the Nile, 'passing with red
pitchers to the river'; Susan 'like an animal with its
eyes near to the ground', 'fell' and 'bestial'; Rhoda
rocking her petals in a brown basin, visiting in her
imagination pools which 'lie on the other side of the
world reflecting marble columns'. The repetition
ensures that we see the characters as distinct entities,
marked by clearly drawn characteristics which do not
change through time. On the other hand, Woolf often
uses metaphors which would suggest that the six
'characters' are to be viewed as aspects of one person.
As Percival arrives in the restaurant, for example,
Bernard (the communicator, the synthesiser) uses
the image of a flower to unite the separate characters:

> There is a red carnation in that vase. A single
> flower as we sat here waiting, but now a seven-sided
> flower, many petalled, red, puce, purple-shaded,
> stiff with silver-tinted leaves – a whole flower to
> which every eye brings its own contribution. (*W*,
> p. 104)

The suggestion is of a multiple subjectivity, with
differences both highlighted and drawn together
through the catalysing presence of Percival. Later in
the text, however, Woolf underscores the fact that the
'characters' when they meet together do not compose
an harmonious 'whole'. It could be argued that in this
text the literal death of Percival operates as a
metaphor for the death of the transcendent subject. It
transpires that his body, like all bodies, can only give
the *illusion* of that self-contained identity which haunts
the narrating consciousness:

> We saw for a moment laid out among us the body of
> the complete human being whom we have failed to
> be, but at the same time, cannot forget. (*W*, p. 231)

Just as Woolf hesitates in this text over fixing identity
as either singular or plural, so too there is a hesitation
over marking the sexual identity of the narrating
consciousness. Woolf's diary notes for the novel stress
the female gender of the narrator, and place the flower
(metaphor, of course, for female sexual identity) at the
centre of her projected text:

> I shall have the two different currents – the moths
> flying along; the flower upright in the centre; a
> perpetual crumbling and renewing of the plant. In
> its leaves she might see things happen. But who is
> she? I am very anxious that she should have no

name. I don't want a Lavinia or a Penelope: I want 'she'.[14]

J. W. Graham, the editor of the holograph drafts of the novel, has also argued that although Woolf frequently disguises the sex of her narrator, this narrator remains recognisably female. He writes that even 'when the narrator has become so attenuated that few readers suspect her existence, her bardic voice continues to deliver [his word] the book'. Yet repeatedly in the manuscript drafts of the text Woolf is explicit about the fact that the sex of the narrator/ perceiver of the novel is immaterial. For example, she writes of 'the lonely person, a man or woman, young or aged, for it does not matter' putting together the fragments of the text and again of the brooding, creating 'mind of the very old person, man or woman . . . it matters not'.[15] In the epigraph to the first draft of the novel, she also offers 'the life of anybody' as a possible title, thus suggesting, again, that the content is not gender-specific. In *The Waves* there is, in comparison with Woolf's earlier novels, a marked *loosening* of automatic gender identifications. 'Feminine' and 'masculine' qualities are no longer so closely tied to physical sexual characteristics, as Woolf moves away from her earlier interest in the (possible) connections between 'femininity' and the female body.

In an essay on *The Waves*, Sara Ruddick considers the question of the gender of the narrator in relation to the memorable 'Elvedon' scene in which the lady sits between 'two long windows, writing'. Ruddick describes her as the female 'teller . . . of the tale', a counterpart, as it were, of the female author of *The Waves*. Although it is tempting to read the passage in this way, I would argue, again, that gender is not the most important element in this key representation.

The lady is first seen by Susan and Bernard as children:

> 'Put your foot on this brick. Look over the wall. That is Elvedon. The lady sits between the two long windows, writing. The gardeners sweep the lawn with giant brooms. We are the first to come here. We are the discoverers of an unknown land. Do not stir: if the gardeners saw us they would shoot us. We should be nailed like stoats to the stable door. Look! Do not move. Grasp the ferns tight on the top of the wall.'
>
> 'I see the lady writing. I see the gardeners sweeping,' said Susan. 'If we died here, nobody would bury us.' (*W*, p. 12)

One of the most striking features of this passage is the sense within it of voyeurism and the breaking of a taboo. Moreover, what seems to be at stake in the children's forbidden looking is death itself ('they would shoot us . . . we should be nailed like stoats'). One of the implications of this passage, then, might be that writing is in some way linked with the forbidden 'primal scene', represented obliquely here through the 'giant brooms sweeping' and through the garden setting. This would seem to link up with the 'Sketch of the Past' fantasy about the origin of the self and of writing discussed earlier in Chapter 1. More importantly, however, the scene is one which seems to underline the *metaphoricity* of writing itself, and this seems to be linked with the element in it of fear. In her essay *Powers of Horror*, Julia Kristeva has a discussion of the process of writing which might shed some light on this. Kristeva links phobia and writing, arguing in a discussion of Freud's 'Little Hans' case history that a phobia (like Hans' fear of horses) constitutes 'a *hieroglyph* that condenses *all fears*, from unnameable to nameable'.[16] In other words, a phobia 'represents', as it were, not just the nameable fears which date from a time after the acquisition of language, but all that which lies 'before' language – 'that conglomeration of fear, deprivation, and nameless frustration, which, properly speaking, belongs to the unnameable'. Following Lacan, Kristeva relates this 'unnameable' fear to 'the *void* upon which rests the play with the signifier and primary processes', and to the 'fundamental fund of anguish' which is masked, Lacan argues, through object relations and language use.

Kristeva goes on to suggest that, in a sense, phobia and language are one, or that, as she puts it, 'the phobic object is a proto-writing'. Like the phobic object, writing 'in the last analysis' refers to fear, 'a terrifying, abject referent'. Kristeva's contention is that most of the time we blank out our knowledge of the phobic and fetishistic nature of language, but that this is something of which the writer is constantly aware. She writes:

> We encounter this discourse in our dreams, or when death brushes us by, depriving us of the assurance mechanical use of speech ordinarily gives us, the assurance of being ourselves, that is, untouchable, unchangeable, immortal. But the writer is permanently confronted with such a language. The writer is a phobic who succeeds in metaphorizing in order to keep from being frightened to death; instead he comes to life again in signs.[17]

It is as though in the Elvedon passage Woolf comes up against the phobic/metaphoric qualities of writing, as she catches herself, as it were, in the act of writing. We are made aware in this passage that writing works not as a reflection of some prior reality, but as a screen which holds off what Kristeva calls 'a dissolving fear'. The passage could even, in Kristevan terms, be read as staging or following an exemplary developmental progression from drive activity (figured through Susan and Bernard) to 'transitional' object relations (figured through the activity of the gardeners) to the purely symbolic activity of speech/writing (figured, of course, through the lady writing). Bernard himself later comments on the importance of the Elvedon episode: it crystallises for him the importance of 'that which is beyond and outside our own predicament ... that which is *symbolic*' (*W*, p. 208, my italics).

In a sense, then, it could be argued that *The Waves* is a novel in which sex and gender boundaries are more fluid or permeable than in some of Woolf's earlier texts. This is one of the features which link it with T. S. Eliot's *The Waste Land*, a text which can productively be read in relation to it. Indeed, *The Waves* is, curiously, the novel of Woolf's which seems to come closest to parallel contemporary texts, while retaining that close web of allusion to earlier literature which marks all her writing. *The Waves* is like *The Waste Land* in having a narrator whose identity (or wholeness) is questioned, and like it too in exploring the possibility (which Freud had made visible) that 'psychic bisexuality' might precede the acquisition of gender identity. Both texts are in touch, too, with a particular kind of psychic distress, figured in *The Waste Land*, famously, through the desert landscape:

> What are the roots that clutch, what branches grow
> Out of this stony rubbish? Son of man,
> You cannot say, or guess, for you know only
> A heap of broken images, where the sun beats,

And the dead tree gives no shelter, the cricket no
   relief,
And the dry stone no sound of water. (I, 19–24)

In *The Waves*, similar imagery is used to figure Rhoda's
pursuit of meaning:

The willow as she saw it grew on the verge of a grey
desert where no bird sang. The leaves shrivelled as
she looked at them, tossed in agony as she passed
them. The trams and omnibuses roared hoarse in
the street, ran over rocks and sped foaming away.
Perhaps one pillar, sunlit, stood in her desert by a
pool where wild beasts come down stealthily to
drink. (*W*, pp. 210–11)

Both texts disclose, perhaps, the ways in which the
social construction of an appropriate self may be
jeopardised by an exploration/acceptance of psychic
bisexuality and of the plurality of identity.

Woolf's text acknowledges Eliot's presence through
the figure of Louis, who, in his role of singular
individual, has characteristics which make him seem
almost like a parody of Eliot. Where Eliot is American,
Louis is Australian; while Eliot worked in a bank,
Louis's father is a banker, and as Gillian Beer
suggests, Louis's 'sordid imagination' and the
particular character of his poetry, seem to be modelled
on those of Eliot. Despite her friendship with Eliot,
Woolf's presentation of the Louis/Eliot figure involves
her in a certain amount of dialogue and critique. In
his aspect as a businessman, Louis, it is suggested,
colludes with the forces of capitalism and imperialism,
both connected by Woolf with patriarchy and 'the
heavy male tread of responsible feet'. More interesting,
perhaps, is Woolf's implied criticism of Louis's

relation to the working classes. Although, as Gillian Beer has argued[18] class is an issue which is not much addressed in *The Waves*, Woolf seems to dramatise her own difficulties in this respect through Louis. Like Woolf, Louis cannot be 'accepted' by the working people with whom he comes into contact: unlike her, he finds it difficult to accept this, and yearns for recognition and inclusion. The reverse side of this coin is Louis's patronising and appropriative attempt to 'redeem' what he perceives to be the squalor of the lives around him, and to incorporate the experience of others into his own. It is significant that Woolf uses the metaphor of a constraining steel ring in this context:

> When I have healed these fractures and comprehended these monstrosities so that they need neither excuse nor apology . . . I shall give back to the street and the eating-shop what they lost when they fell on these hard times . . . I shall assemble a few words and forge round us a hammered ring of beaten steel. (*W*, pp. 139–40)

Another text which has an intertextual relation to *The Waves* is Katherine Mansfield's long story 'At the Bay', first published, like *The Waste Land*, in 1922. 'At the Bay' has a structure which has some similarities with that of *The Waves*. Its time span is that of one day, rather than the more complex day/life-span of *The Waves*, but within the constraints of the single day setting, Mansfield explores, like Woolf, the cycles of life and death. 'At the Bay' begins, like *The Waves*, with the borderline between land and sea – 'The sun was not yet risen . . . there was nothing to mark which was beach and where was the sea'.[19] The early morning setting suggests an analogy with the birth of the subject, and this parallel between the passage of the day and the cycle of human life is sustained throughout Mansfield's text. 'At the Bay' might have suggested, then, something of the central image and structure of *The Waves*, just as Mansfield's earlier story *Prelude* (published by the Hogarth Press) might have offered one of the models for *To the Lighthouse*, with its domestic setting, use of the house as a psychic structure, and the presence of an ambivalent (phallic?) title image (*Prelude* was originally called 'The Aloe').

Apart from the similarities in construction and technique, the deeper similarity between *The Waves* and 'At the Bay' lies in the ways in which both texts broach what Françoise Defromont has called 'the reality, and indeed the haunting questions, of death'.[20] In both texts, we are aware, continually, of 'death brushing us by', to repeat Kristeva's evocative phrase. In 'At the Bay', death enters the text explicitly in the scene between Kezia and her grandmother (Section VII), when the grandmother's knowledge of death intersects, momentarily and shockingly, with Kezia's youthful obliviousness. But an awareness of death always at the borders of life is there throughout the text, conveyed through the lightest of touches (Stanley racing 'for dear life' down to the sea to bathe; the description of the 'quick dark . . . racing over the sea, over the sandhills'). In both 'At the Bay' and *The Waves*, we are always aware of an unspeakable void 'behind' the screen of activity, pattern and colour which constitutes the text. Returning to Kristeva's discussion of phobia, one could argue that for both Woolf and Mansfield, writing holds off both the fear which constitutes the subject and the death which is the ultimate referent of the fear. In *The Waves*, this complexity is suggested, perhaps, through the double negative of its ending. The last word of the narrative (which was originally to have suggested, in Woolf's words, 'that the theme effort, effort, dominates: not the waves') is in fact, of course, 'Death', and the last line of the text returns us to the fall of the waves which figure, if our beginning, certainly also our end.

The Years

Like *The Waves*, *The Years* is a text which is preoccupied with time, mortality and the cycle(s) of life. However, *The Years* moves away from the particular concentration of *The Waves* and its focus on the ambiguities of one controlling metaphor (birth/death). Instead, *The Years* is a text which explores the social forces which construct the 'realities' of its characters. Woolf made a decision in this novel to explore the relation between private experience and its wider social contexts, writing to Stephen Spender that she had, she felt, if anything, sacrificed the private to the public in this novel:

> I expect I muted the characters down too much, in order to shorten and keep their faces towards society; and altogether muffled the proportions: which should have given a round, not a thin line.[21]

For many years after its first publication, critics tended to concur with Woolf's implicitly negative view of the text, a view based on the assumption that there ought to be some sort of balance between 'fact' and 'vision', or what Mitchell Leaska calls 'granite' and 'rainbow', in a novel.[22] More recently, feminist critics such as Jane Marcus have rescued *The Years* from relative critical neglect, and have argued that in both *The Years* and in *Three Guineas* Woolf produces a

brilliant political analysis of her time, a sustained
critique of the institutions of patriarchy, capitalism
and Empire. What these recent critics have not
sufficiently brought out, however, is the very marked
shift in *The Years* from 'vision' to 'fact', a shift brought
about – despite Woolf's own hesitations and dis-
claimers – because she was more interested in this
novel in the *construction* of experience than in experience 'for itself'. In other words, *The Years* seems to
indicate a move on Woolf's part towards a (post)
modern perspective like that described by Richard
Rorty:

> The line of thought common to Blumenberg,
> Nietzsche, Freud and Davidson suggests that we try
> to get to the point where we no longer worship
> *anything*, where we treat *nothing* as a quasi divinity,
> where we treat *everything* – our language, our
> conscience, our community – as a product of time
> and chance.[23]

The shift in Woolf's work from 'vision' to 'fact' marks
a move in her work from a sense of the possibility of
transcendent meaning(s) towards a sense of radical
contingency. This seems to place *The Years* with
Between the Acts as a postmodern text, as indeed Alan
Wilde has argued in his study of the connections
between modernism and postmodernism.[24] It also
involves an emphasis on history and change which is
unlike anything in Woolf's earlier fiction. She wrote of
her aim in this respect to Stephen Spender:

> What I meant I think was to give a picture of
> society as a whole ... envelop the whole in a
> changing temporal atmosphere ... show the old
> fabric insensibly changing without death or violence

into the future – suggesting that there is no break, but a continuous development . . .[25]

The major 'theme' of *The Years* (less a theme than a point of departure) is a radical critique of family life. In charting the history of the Pargiter family from 1880 to the 1930s, Woolf does more than note the horrors of family life in relation to specific issues such as child abuse, the oppression of unmarried daughters and so on. She offers a critique of the institution of the family in a wider social and philosophical context, and this links *The Years* closely with *A Room of One's Own* and *Three Guineas*. One can also compare Woolf's understanding of the contingency but also the pervasive power of family structures with Foucault's analysis of the pivotal role of the family in the organisation of the modern state. In the first volume of *The History of Sexuality*, Foucault analyses the operation of 'sexuality' as a system of discourse and power, and focuses on the ways in which family structures support 'a few major strategies' of knowledge and power:

the family organization, precisely to the extent that it was insular and heteromorphous with respect to the other power mechanisms, was used to support the great 'maneuvers' employed for the Malthusian control of the birthrate, for the populationist incitements, for the medicalization of sex and the psychiatrization of its nongenital forms.[26]

Woolf, like Foucault, analyses the ways in which the family controls the experience of its members in relation to what she calls 'love' and in relation to money. Moreover, in *The Pargiters* (the essay-novel which formed the basis for the first part of *The Years*), her discussion of 'drawing-room love' and 'street love' takes her very close to Foucauldian thought as she traces the ways in which the (presumed) existence of a predatory male sexuality exerts particular pressures on the female members of the family:

> Nothing perhaps influenced the lives of the Pargiters in March 1880 more powerfully and more completely than the principle of that love which – to distinguish it from the different loves of the drawing room – may be called street love, common love, love in general. This love affected the lives of the girls far more strongly than it affected the lives of their brothers . . . A large radius of the West End indeed was closed to them, whether by day or by night, unless they went with a brother or their mother; and even the hansom cab, in which they were forced to make their transit of the dangerous area, had to have both flaps of its door shut.[27]

The comic exaggeration of tone signals Woolf's sense of the preposterous, constructed nature of this sexuality, this 'street love', which was in a sense instituted and solicited by the very structures which officially aimed to repress it. Woolf's understanding thus accords with Foucault's view that sexuality is a constructed discursive field, part of a network of power relations, and that the social rules which ostensibly aim to 'repress' sexuality (like the rules which govern the lives of the Pargiter girls) in fact construct and incite the appropriate 'sexual' feeling. So in *The Pargiters* we become aware of the ways in which social conventions construct an embarrassed but (crucially) compliant response to the male body for Delia and Milly:

> Both Delia and Milly blushed with a peculiar shame when Eleanor said 'Don't be caught looking'

– they wanted to look at the young man; they knew
it was wrong to look; they did look; they were
caught looking; they disliked being caught; they
were ashamed, indignant, confused – all in one –
(*P*, p. 38)

If Foucault's work has focused on the construction of
sexuality (and on the social structures associated with
it) in a fairly broad sense, feminist thinkers have
focused more particularly on the reproductive elements
of family life, and hence on what Adrienne Rich calls
the role of 'compulsory heterosexuality' in Western
society. This too is brought into focus in *The Years*,
which contrasts the solid structure of Victorian family
life, in which divergent sexualities are denied, with the
more flexible practices of the post-war world, in which
'different loves' are to some extent accommodated. In
following the lives of Rose and Sara Pargiter, as we
shall see, Woolf registers the ways in which the
institution of compulsory heterosexuality (with the
system of a-symmetrical gender relations which it
implies) can be contested by 'outsider' figures (such as
Rose) who choose different living arrangements:

the years after all – she was over forty – made one
care very little what people thought. They used to
say, why don't you marry? Why don't you do this or
that, interfering. But not any longer.[28]

Woolf's radical critique of family life finds its most
direct expression through North's observations at
Delia's party. North is a key 'outsider' figure,
scrutinising the Pargiters after an absence of several
years in Africa. Effectively detached from his family,
North finds the workings of family life, and the
organisation of all experience in and through the
family, strange and indeed fearful to contemplate:

That was what it came to – thirty years of being husband and wife – tut-tut-tut – and chew-chew-chew. It sounded like the half-inarticulate munchings of animals in a stall . . .

They were inviting him to stay with them at the Towers in September for cub-hunting. The men shot, and the women – he looked at his aunt as if she might be breaking into young even there, on that chair – the women broke off into innumerable babies. And those babies had other babies . . . He was sinking; he was falling under their weight; the name in his pocket even was fading. Could nothing be done about it? he asked himself. Nothing short of revolution, he thought. (*Y*, p. 356)

North associates the family with reproduction in two senses. He sees sexuality as expressed in marriage as both bestial and degrading, and thus views the production of children with distaste (he later connects propagation with egotism). The reference to cub-hunting also serves to underline the coercive power of 'packs', which stand as a metaphor for the family. But North also sees the more intangible coercion of family life, the ways in which it 'reproduces' the same categories of subjectivity/subjection over a period of time. It is this ideological reproduction – this continued production of subjects obedient to existing power-relations – which can, he thinks, only be challenged by 'revolution'.

In a subsequent passage, North reflects on the ways in which 'the family' (patriarchy working through compulsory heterosexuality) 'rounds' subjects into 'identity'. Again, there is a strategic ambivalence here: the word 'identity' suggests both individualism (the ego) and conformity. The suggestion is that individuals reproduce themselves in order to maintain or extend

their goods and property, their 'stake' in the world.
Egotism rather than altruism is the driving force – and
force is the operative word. Again, metaphors of
coercion are deployed:

> North fidgeted. This is the conspiracy, he said to
> himself; this is the steam roller that smooths,
> obliterates; rounds into identity; rolls into balls. He
> listened. Jimmy was in Uganda; Lily was in
> Leicestershire; *my* boy – *my* girl . . . they were
> saying. But they're not interested in other people's
> children, he observed. Only in their own; their own
> property; their own flesh and blood, which they
> would protect with the unsheathed claws of the
> primeval swamp, he thought, looking at Milly's fat
> little paws, even Maggie, even she. For she too was
> talking about my boy, my girl. How then can we be
> civilised, he asked himself? (*Y*, p. 359)

Woolf traces coercion too in the workings of the strict
taboos which structure compulsory heterosexuality/
family life. *The Years* is notable for its exploration of
incest and homosexuality, both topics, of course,
which it was difficult to broach in the 1930s. Woolf's
own experience of incest has been charted briefly in
Chapter 1: as we have seen, it is likely that Woolf was
abused by both her half-brothers, Gerald and George
Duckworth, and that the abuse began when she was
about six years old. Because of her childhood experiences, Woolf may have experienced some difficulty in
writing of incest, but it remains a powerful, if partly
suppressed, theme in *The Years*. In the novel, Woolf
shows incest to be an integral part of extended family
life. Incestuous relationships exist across the three
generations of the Pargiter family, between father and
daughters, between siblings and between cousins.

Incestuous attachments exist, for example, between Abel and Eugenie, Martin and Maggie, and Peggy and Morris. However, it is in Woolf's choice of a metaphor for incest, rather than in the delineation of a particular relationship, that her understanding of the working of the incest taboo is most clearly demonstrated. Woolf's metaphor for incest comes from Sophocles, from the same source as Freud's Oedipus complex. Rather than focusing on Oedipus, however, Woolf concentrates on Antigone, Oedipus's daughter. In a key scene in the novel, Sara Pargiter is reading from her cousin Edward's translation of *Antigone*, and, at the same time, paying half-hearted attention to a party outside, with the endless comings and goings of dancing couples. The juxtaposition of Antigone's story, with its extremes of feeling, and the mechanical pairing of the dancing partners mirrors the clash of values in Sophocles' play between the character who goes against the law and the pragmatists and conformists. Antigone, of course, forgoes marriage and children in order to bury her brother: she sets herself outside the law, directing her feelings to her brother and her incestuous parents, rather than towards Creon and the state. Antigone is thus connected with a current of incestuous feeling which seems to run outside the law and to oppose it, and Sara Pargiter, in turn, is identified with Antigone:

The man in the loincloth gave three sharp taps with his mallet on the brick. She was buried alive. The tomb was a brick mound. There was just room for her to lie straight out. Straight out in a brick tomb, she said. And that's the end, she yawned, shutting the book.

She laid herself out, under the cold smooth sheets, and pulled the pillow over her ears. The one sheet and the one blanket fitted softly round her. (*Y*, p. 131)

The point, of course, is partly that Antigone's being buried alive is not 'the end': she subsequently hangs herself in the tomb, and two more deaths follow. But despite the effect of these tragedies, the emphasis in Sophocles' play is finally on the power of (social) law, embodied in the pragmatist Creon and exemplified in the punishment of Antigone (and Oedipus before her). Woolf's choice of text thus suggests an understanding of the fact that the incest taboo (structurally necessary, Lévi-Strauss argues, for the institution of patriarchy/ heterosexuality) may be important less for its suppression of incest (which, Foucault argues, it actually incites) than for its ability to demonstrate and consolidate the power of the law.

In *The Years*, Woolf is thus ambivalent about the effect or efficacy of the breaking of social taboos. Sara Pargiter, for example, is associated with incest through her devotion to her sister Maggie (their relationship has parallels with that between Virginia Woolf and Vanessa Bell). She is also connected with homosexuality through her love for Nicholas, a man who, in turn, loves, as she explains to Eleanor, 'the other sex, the other sex, you see'. However, Nicholas's *status* in the text is rather difficult to determine. While Eleanor approves of him, North thinks he is 'a bit of a – shall we say "bounder"?'. He is also shown to be an ineffectual figure, making almost exactly the same conversational moves over the space of twenty years, and being unable to give the speech which he wants to give at the end of Delia's party. The other character who is associated with homosexuality, Rose, is however far more positively presented in the text. Rose's name, of course, is significant: the rose is the flower which, as we have seen, often functions as a metaphor for female sexuality for Woolf, and it is also, significantly, Rose's mother's name. Rose is therefore connected with a female sexuality which is 'woman-identified', or woman-centred Such sexuality need not be specifically tied to lesbianism (although in this case it is): it can also exist in the context of a more diffuse celebration of 'feminine' sexuality, as in *Mrs Dalloway*.

Rose's lesbianism is seen by Sara Pargiter, at least, as constituting a significant threat to the Pargiters and to the reproduction of conventional family life. Rose is often associated with military metaphors: as a child she thinks of herself in a private game as 'Pargiter of Pargiter's Horse', riding to the rescue of a besieged garrison, and her identification with the male role may be seen as a challenge to established values. Many years later, her cousin Sara views Rose in terms which echo the childhood game, and which again place Rose in opposition to the unthinking reproduction of family life:

> 'It's not ordinary,' she said. 'The Pargiters –' She was holding a fork in her hand, and she drew a line on the table-cloth. 'The Pargiters,' she repeated, 'going on and on and on' – here her fork touched a salt-cellar – 'until they came to a rock,' she said; 'and then Rose' – she looked at her again: Rose drew herself up slightly, '– Rose claps spurs to her horse, rides straight up to a man in a gold coat, and says "Damn your eyes!" ' (*Y*, p. 161)

The 'rock' on which the Pargiters founder might be that 'bedrock' of which Freud wrote in an essay published in the same year as *The Years*,[29] the bedrock of femininity which will, according to Freud, be repudiated both by the 'normal' man and by the woman who remains masculine. Femininity, in all its constructed impossibility, is decisively repudiated by Rose, who later, of course, becomes a militant suffragette who is imprisoned and force-fed for her pains.

Rose's rejection of the feminine role which is by Freud's own account so difficult to sustain may be seen as a qualified success: her way of living can be seen as in some sense a subversion of established codes and expectations. But on the whole in *The Years* the reader is extremely conscious of the 'weight' of social pressure 'sinking' the life of the individual, muffling him or her and preventing change.

One of the ways in which Woolf explores this pressure is through the metaphor of the house, which is, so to speak, structural in this novel. While the feminist critic Susan Squier has written on the importance of the city as a metaphor in *The Years*,[30] the metaphor of the house has been less fully explored. The house operates in *The Years* as a metaphor for female identity, and in this respect Woolf's novel is close to other 'domestic' novels of the 1930s by writers such as Elizabeth Bowen and Rosamond Lehmann. Woolf emphasises in *The Years* that domestic life constrains women both literally and metaphorically. In the 'Second Essay' of *The Pargiters*, she comments on the extraordinary circumscription of the lives of the Pargiter girls, 'sitting round a tea table with nothing better to do than to change the sheets at Whiteleys', and in the finished text of *The Years* we have the following description of the Pargiter drawing room:

> Then she went, creaking in her cheap shoes, to the window and drew the curtains. They slid with a familiar click along the brass rod, and soon the

windows were obscured by thick sculptured folds of
claret-coloured plush. When she had drawn the
curtains in both rooms, a profound silence seemed
to fall upon the drawing-room. The world outside
seemed thickly and entirely cut off ... For a
moment wheels ground on the road; then they died
out and the silence was complete. (*Y*, p. 19)

The description echoes that of the red room in *Jane
Eyre*, with its drawn red curtains and sculptured
drapery: the use of the words 'obscured', 'thickly' and
'silence' increases the sense in this passage of (female)
domestic life as claustrophobic, even tomb-like. The
house thus figures the physical and ideological constraints on women's existence in the Victorian and
early modern period. The house is also closely
identified with the female body. Like the female body/
female identity, the house accommodates male
sexuality/male identity, but also shuts it out: female
domestic space thus offers a *compromised* autonomy, as
in classic Victorian 'separate spheres' ideology.

We can see the house working as a kind of
equivalent for the female body in Woolf's treatment of
Eugenie, Lady Pargiter. After her death, Martin
thinks of Eugenie as though she were literally conterminous with her house (' "I liked her," he said. "I
liked going there." He saw the untidy room; the piano
open . . .'). In an earlier and very striking, scene, the
metaphors of the flower for female sexuality and of the
house for the female body are brought together. As
Eugenie dances for her daughters after a party, her
body is likened to a flower, in a manner reminiscent of
Woolf's descriptions of Mrs Ramsay ('Her body
seemed to fold and close itself together as she sighed').
She then promises to tell her daughters 'the story of
the bouquet', a story connected with a romantic

escapade in her youth (this might remind us of Mrs Dalloway and Sally Seton). However, her husband intervenes, and Eugenie is reprimanded because she has neglected to lock up the house properly:

> Then she heard the voices of her father and mother as they came up the kitchen stairs. They had been down in the basement; there had been a burglary up the street; her mother had promised to have a new lock put on the kitchen door but had forgotten. She could hear her father say:
> '. . . they'd melt it down; we should never get it back again.' (*Y*, p. 139)

In this short scene, Eugenie moves from identification with dance and flower to identification with the house as property which, like her body, must be guarded and controlled. In this passage of apparently 'realistic' description, Woolf thus suggests a sharp contrast between an autonomous female sexuality which is open and full of possibilities, and the closed (or locked) 'house of love' which women inhabit in patriarchy.

As the metaphor of the house economically suggests, Woolf focuses attention in *The Years* on the way in which female identity is *constructed*. A passage from the speech given before the London/National Society for Women's Service (in which both *The Years* and the famous essay 'Professions for Women' originated) makes this point very clearly. Woolf is describing the 'Angel in the House':

> Now this creature – it was one of her most annoying characteristics – never had any real existence. She had – what is much more difficult to deal with – an ideal existence, a fictitious existence. She was a

dream, a phantom – a kind of mirage like the pools and the palm trees which nature places in the desert to lure the caravan across. The Angel in the house was the ideal of womanhood created by the imaginations of men and women at a certain stage of their pilgrimage to lure them across a very dusty stretch (of the journey). They agreed to accept this ideal, because for reasons I cannot now go into – they have to do with the British Empire, our colonies, Queen Victoria, Lord Tennyson, the growth of the middle class and so on – [reality] (a real relationship) between men and woman was then unattainable.[31]

Woolf's metaphors of the 'mirage' and the 'ideal' place in a critical perspective the *idealised* 'feminine identity' which is so important in *Mrs Dalloway* and *To the Lighthouse*. In this passage, Woolf stresses the contingency of the construction of such identity 'at a certain stage' in history. She is explicit too about the social and economic forces which produced a particular set of gender-identifications in the Victorian period. Such a sense of history and contingency implies, of course, the possibility of change, which is both shown (in 'The Present Day') and envisaged for the future in *The Years*.

Change is brought about principally through the loosening of family structures. This is imaged in *The Years* through the break-up of family homes. Once Abercorn Terrace and Browne Street have been sold, we see few family houses in this text (Morris's mother-in-law's house and Maggie and Renny's small home are exceptions). Instead, the Pargiter siblings disperse to live in flats and rented rooms, often in unsavoury areas. By the end of the novel, Delia is, it seems, living in a flat above offices. So Woolf registers economic and social change, as we see the large houses required for the extended Victorian family being converted, first into flats and then (with the growth of the suburbs) into offices.

Family homes disappear from the text partly because so many of the younger Pargiters remain unmarried. Again, the text reflects demographic change here, and especially the increase in the numbers of single women living on their own. Eleanor is representative here, her 'new shower-bath' the image of her hard-won emotional and physical independence. Martin also lives alone, keeping a mistress in Kensington, while Rose lives first with a lover, and then alone. Edward's collegiate existence suits his liking (if not love) for his own sex. Of the siblings who marry we learn relatively little, but Milly and Hugh are the object of North's fierce critique, as noted above. Indeed, Woolf presents the break-up of traditional family life as an unequivocal gain, for it leads to lives of greater independence and less hypocrisy, as Martin suggests:

It was an abominable system, he thought; family life; Abercorn Terrace. No wonder the house would not let. It had one bathroom, and a basement; and there all those different people had lived, boxed up together, telling lies. (*Y*, p. 212)

In resisting domestic life and patriarchal structures of reproduction, the younger generation open up the way to new concepts of identity, crossing or going beyond gender stereotypes. This is especially marked in the relationship between Sara (a key figure, and also a writer, in the draft of *The Pargiters*) and Nicholas 'Brown' (replacing Browne Street). Sara and Nicholas (perhaps loosely based on the characters of Dora

Carrington and Lytton Strachey) point the way to 'different loves' which are not based on a conventional alignment of sex, gender and identity:

> This is their love-making, Eleanor thought, half listening to their laughter, to their bickering. Another inch of the pattern, she thought, still using her half-formulated ideas to stamp the immediate scene. And if this love-making differs from the old, still it has its charm; it was 'love', different from the old love, perhaps, but worse, was it? Anyhow, she thought, they are aware of each other; they live in each other; what else is love, she asked, listening to their laughter. (*Y*, pp. 351–2)

Woolf here explores the possibility of 'breaking the sequence' of sex/gender/identity, calling into question the 'natural' relation between these three categories. In other words, sex and gender need not necessarily be aligned (we are now of course familiar with this argument); nor need gender and identity be so aligned. Driving a wedge between gender and identity is a radical move, for it is largely through the category of gender that the concept of a homogeneous and coherent self is maintained.

It is through the third generation of Pargiters especially, through North and Peggy, that Woolf expresses hope for the future via a redefinition of one's identity and relationship to others. North, in particular, rejects a political or external route to change, in terms which may seem vaguely Forsterian (i.e. liberal rather than radical) until we notice his rejection of a 'desirable residence with its three-quarters of an acre of garden', i.e. of family structure, as well as his radical emphasis on reconstruction from within:

But he did not believe in joining societies, in signing
manifestoes. He turned back to the desirable
residence with its three-quarters of an acre of
garden and running water in all the bedrooms.
People met, he thought, pretending to read, in hired
halls. And one of them stood on a platform. There
was the pump-handle gesture; the wringing-wet-
clothes gesture; and then the voice, oddly detached
from the little figure and tremendously magnified
by the loudspeaker, went booming and bawling
round the hall: Justice! Liberty! . . . Something's
wrong, he thought; there's a gap, a dislocation,
between the word and the reality. If they want to
reform the world, he thought, why not begin there,
at the centre, with themselves? (*Y*, pp. 384–5, my
italics)

North is preoccupied with ways of rethinking the
relation between self and other in a manner
reminiscent of Bernard in *The Waves*. He too contemplates a 'world without a self', and then re-
considers, and thinks rather of ways of reconciling self
and other, of retaining identity (or difference) without
imposing it on others:

Not black shirts, green shirts, red shirts – always
posing in the public eye; that's all poppycock. Why
not down barriers and simplify? But a world, he
thought, that was all one jelly, one mass, would be a
rice pudding world, a white counterpane world. To
keep the emblems and tokens of North Pargiter –
the man Maggie laughs at; the Frenchman holding
his hat; but at the same time spread out, make a
new ripple in human consciousness, be the bubble
and the stream, the stream and the bubble – myself
and the world together – he raised his glass.

Anonymously, he said, looking at the clear yellow
liquid. (*Y*, pp. 389–90)

North's sense that the relation between self and other,
subject and object must be reconstructed if 'revolution'
is to occur is close to the thought of postmodern
feminists such as Hélène Cixous and Julia Kristeva.
For both Cixous and Kristeva, subjectivity must be
renegotiated if social change is to occur. For Kristeva,
difference must not be externalised but confronted
from within so that, as she puts it:

the struggle, the implacable difference, the violence
be conceived in the very place where it operates
with the maximum intransigence, in other words, in
personal and sexual identity itself, so as to make it
disintegrate in its very nucleus.[32]

Cixous, putting it rather differently ('and in ways
which are closer to Woolf) expresses a similar sense of
the need to reconsider the relation between subject
and object if changes in social relations are to be
brought about:

One could, in fact, imagine that difference or
inequality – if one understands by that noncoincid-
ence, asymmetry – lead to desire without negativity,
without one of the partner's succumbing: we would
recognise each other in a type of exchange in which
each one would keep the *other* alive and different.[33]

The possibility of difference in another sense, i.e. as
change, is kept before us in *The Years* through North
and Peggy. Both characters repeatedly express their
sense of the need to 'live differently, differently'.
Though Peggy finds it difficult to put into words, her

shadowy conception of the new is recognised by North and understood to be the counterpart of his own vision:

> He felt her feeling now; it was not about him; it was about other people; about another world, a new world . . . (*Y*, p. 401)

Such a vision of the new also finds expression in *The Years* through the song which the caretaker's children sing at the very end of the text, just before the dawn. It is incomprehensible to the middle-class guests at Delia's party:

> Nobody knew what to say. There was something horrible in the noise they made. It was so shrill, so discordant, and so meaningless. (*Y*, p. 409)

Joanna Lipking has suggested that the song is the expression of a 'divine spirit' beyond or outside history: Jane Marcus describes the song as 'Latin words and Cockney English mixed with echoes of Greek'. It is interesting to note that (without any glossary being available, of course) the words *sound* like verbs being conjugated or substituted one for the other ('Mai to, kai to, lai to see' . . .). Does the rudimentary song suggest then that the *ground* of meaning lies not in substantives, but in processes and relations, thus presenting us in miniature with a thesis which has driven the whole book? Throughout *The Years* Woolf emphasises the fact that there are no fixed truths, only relations, and that truth is context-specific. So the children's song sounds 'hideous' in its present context, but may be capable of different interpretations in the future. Moreover, Eleanor's divided response to the song underlines that fact that we can only respond positively to things which we have been culturally conditioned to perceive. Eleanor can recognise the children's (childish) beauty and innocence, and can map that onto an internal mental grid, but has no experience which will help her to decode their song. She is a character, however, who remains open to change, and as such might be seen as a model for the ideal reader at the end of this radical text:

> The contrast between their faces and their voices was astonishing; it was impossible to find one word for the whole. 'Beautiful?' she said, with a note of interrogation, turning to Maggie.
> 'Extraordinarily,' said Maggie.
> But Eleanor was not sure that they were thinking of the same thing. (*Y*, p. 409)

6 Coins and Mirrors: *Three Guineas* and *Between the Acts*

Three Guineas

Three Guineas is the text by Woolf which aroused most opposition in her lifetime, particularly from other members of 'the Bloomsbury Group', for example Maynard Keynes, who thought the book 'a silly argument and not very well written'. While some of her friends criticised it for its feminism, the book came in for criticism from other quarters because it was thought elitist, paying too little attention to the lives of working-class women. More recently, the book has been taken up by American feminist critics of the 1980s and used as evidence for Woolf's radical feminism and understanding of the violence inherent in patriarchal culture. In *Three Guineas* Woolf argues for the connection between the political repressiveness of Fascism and the in-built oppression of patriarchy, suggesting that in a sense the one is a consequence of the other, for 'the public and the private worlds are inseparably connected'. She was one of the first to see that the oppression of women, and the reduction of women to their sexual and reproductive functions, was crucial to the Fascist programme. In *Three Guineas* she anatomises fascist rhetoric in the following way, alert to and wary of the use of 'nature' to legitimate patriarchal/fascist ideology:

The nature of manhood and the nature of womanhood are frequently defined both by Italian and
German dictators. Both repeatedly insist that it is
the nature of man and indeed the essence of
manhood to fight. Hitler, for example, draws a
distinction between 'a nation of pacifists and a
nation of men'. Both repeatedly insist that it is the
nature of womanhood to heal the wounds of the
fighter. Nevertheless a very strong movement is on
foot towards emancipating men from the old
'natural and eternal law' that man is essentially a
fighter.[1]

In this passage, Woolf spells out that distinction
between sex and gender which she is sometimes
accused of blurring. Indeed, as we have seen, from
Orlando onwards one of Woolf's main concerns is an
exploration of the ways in which gendered identity is
constructed and imposed in order to ensure the
continuing (pre)dominance of men. In *Orlando* and *A
Room of One's Own* she stresses the lack of fit between
the restrictions of gender and the fullness of early
psychic life; in *The Years* she explores the institutions
and mechanisms (the family, in particular) which
ensure the reproduction of gender/patriarchy. In *Three
Guineas*, however, Woolf confronts head on the
question of change. The essay circles round the
question of how changes in gender relations can be
effected. The circular method reflects, perhaps, the
fact that Woolf finds fewer certain answers than some
of her more optimistic feminist critics.

In *Three Guineas*, Woolf continues the work of *The
Years* in analysing the structures and institutions of
patriarchy. This is unsurprising, as the texts are
thought to have originated together in Woolf's idea for
'an entire new book – a sequel to a Room of One's

Own – about the sexual life of women'.[2] As in *The Years*, the private house is a central image in *Three Guineas*, functioning as both symbol and agent of repressive 'separate spheres' ideology. Early titles for the essay included *The Open Door* and *Opening the Door*, and as Susan Squier has pointed out, the image of a door opening and a woman crossing a bridge between the private and public worlds is a central one in this text. Woolf vividly evokes the repressive atmosphere of 'the private house', and in terms reminiscent of *The Years* emphasises the ways in which female subjectivity was/is produced and defined by the possibilities of the domestic sphere:

> It was with a view to marriage that she tinkled on the piano, but was not allowed to join an orchestra; sketched innocent domestic scenes, but was not allowed to study from the nude; read this book, but was not allowed to read that, charmed, and talked. (*TG*, p. 206)

Woman's role as sacred vessel, the bearer of (one) man's children and of his name, means that she must be immured in the private house, first of her father then of her husband. The possibility of 'stepping out' is held before us, tantalisingly, in *Three Guineas*, but it remains a possibility only. Woolf argues that this is because women have no real opportunities of employment outside marriage. Without economic independence there can be no freedom of expression, and no real possibility of contesting patriarchy and its values. Indeed, Woolf argues that in these (negative) circumstances women will support the very values which constrain them, to the point of endorsing war outside the home as well as within it. So Woolf writes of the woman whose education remains that of the 'private house':

Consciously she must use whatever charm or beauty she possessed to flatter and cajole the busy men, the soldiers, the lawyers, the ambassadors, the cabinet ministers who wanted recreation after their day's work. Consciously she must accept their views, and fall in with their decrees because it was only so that she could wheedle them into giving her the means to marry or marriage itself. (*TG*, p. 207)

Woolf suggests, then, that women's marginality is self-perpetuating, in political, and also in ideological terms. One of the most striking features of the opening of *Three Guineas* is Woolf's description of photographs of the Spanish Civil War, in which we see 'dead bodies' and 'the section of a house':

A bomb has torn open the side; there is still a birdcage hanging in what was presumably the sitting-room, but the rest of the house looks like nothing so much as a bunch of spillikins suspended in mid-air. (*TG*, p. 164)

Throughout the text, Woolf returns to these pictures of ruined houses: they are a touchstone in her reflections on how to stop war and in her meditations on the relationship between patriarchy and fascism. This leaves the reader, however, facing the difficulty that while Woolf calls on women to leave the private house in *Three Guineas*, it seems that their efforts are required only to protect and perpetuate the (re)building of other private houses. There is a circularity in the imagery here which seems to point to a critical impasse. It is as though women are trapped in ideological and imaginative as well as political terms, prevented from imagining alternative ways of being/living.

Woolf is very clear in *Three Guineas* that marriage is, at best, a profession (although it is not well paid); at worst, prostitution. In other words, she focuses on the economic, as well as on the practical and ideological structures of patriarchy. As she points out, the work of women, in all its various aspects, is grossly underpaid. Again, however, there is ambiguity. Woolf touches on the political point that if women's work were to be waged, capitalism would be put under severe pressure. She notes that without the (unpaid) work of 'wives and mothers and daughters', 'the State would collapse and fall to pieces'. On the other hand, she argues somewhat disingenuously that proper payment for motherhood and childcare would 'ease the burden' for men, who would then not have to work such long hours to support wives and children:

> For if your wife were paid for her work, the work of bearing and bringing up children, a real wage, a money wage, so that it became an attractive profession instead of being as it is now an unpaid profession, an unpensioned profession, and therefore a precarious and dishonoured profession, your own slavery would be lightened. (*TG*, p. 317)

The problem which is elided is that of where the money is to come from. In fact there is no money, no surplus: in economic, as in ideological terms, there is no 'give' in the system, no new space or source from which that system can be regenerated. Repeatedly in *Three Guineas* a narrative drive towards the 'imagination of the new' comes up against this kind of limit or impasse.

Woolf also explores the psychic limits restricting women's 'freedom'. For the first time, she uses Freud explicitly, drawing on references to his work in a pamphlet commissioned by the Church of England to enquire into 'the development of the Ministry of Women' (*The Ministry of Women: Report of the Archbishops' Commission*, 1935). She quotes from a certain Professor Grensted, who used Freudian concepts to explain male hostility to the ordination of women. Professor Grensted writes of the 'strong emotion with which this whole subject is commonly approached', and notes that:

> whatever be the exact value and interpretation of the material upon which theories of the 'Oedipus complex' and the 'castration complex' have been founded, it is clear that the general acceptance of male dominance, and still more of feminine inferiority, resting upon subconscious ideas of women as 'man manqué', has its background in infantile conceptions of this type. These commonly, and even usually, survive in the adult, despite their irrationality. (*TG*, pp. 339–40)

We might compare Freud, in a paper translated by James Strachey in 1927, on the little boy's (retroactive) response to his first sight of the female genitals. Freud notes two reactions which may 'permanently determine the boy's relations to women: horror of the mutilated creature or triumphant contempt for her'.[3]

By incorporating Freudian material into her analysis of male hostility/dominance, Woolf underscores the similarity (or convergence) between her understanding of gender and that of Freud. As we have seen, her texts explore many aspects of the process whereby the fullness of pre-Oedipal existence is 'converted', via the Oedipal crisis, into the rigidity of gender identity. Repeatedly, her texts stress the importance of mother–daughter and/or same-sex relations in alleviating the pain of the girl child's passage into 'fully' gendered femininity, and repeatedly, too, they challenge the arbitrary construction of gender identities. In *Three Guineas*, Woolf stresses the irrational nature of the 'sex-taboo' described by Grensted and stresses too the absurdity of erecting gender categories simply on the basis of anatomical differences.

Implicit in both Woolf and Freud's understanding of sexual difference is the sense that the passage through the Oedipal crisis compromises both male and female subjects, bringing about a diminution rather than an increase in possibilities of experience/ expression. (This point is developed further, of course, by Lacan, who stresses the 'alienated' condition of both male and female subjects in the symbolic order.) In *Three Guineas*, Woolf uses a striking metaphor to suggest the cost involved in the accession to gendered identity. In the following passage she suggests initially that 'society' is kinder to men, but then her use of the image of the 'private brother' complicates the issue. She writes:

> Inevitably we look upon societies as conspiracies that sink the private brother, whom many of us have reason to respect, and inflate in his stead a monstrous male, loud of voice, hard of fist, childishly intent upon scoring the floor of the earth with chalk marks, within whose mystic boundaries human beings are penned, rigidly, separately, artificially; where, daubed red and gold, decorated like a savage with feathers he goes through mystic rites and enjoys the dubious pleasures of power and dominion while we, 'his' women, are locked in the private house without share in the many societies of which his society is composed. (*TG*, p. 308)

The private brother could figure that element of the 'self' which must be repressed in the acquisition of 'feminine' identity, and/or that element in the male subject which must be repressed in the acquisition of 'masculine' identity. The second interpretation seems the more likely in view of the connexions which are made here between private and public aggression, and the extrapolation from the 'hard fist' of the brother to the 'rigid' (but 'artificial') boundaries of imperialism. Woolf thus suggests that there is a cost for men too in the acquisition of that 'masculinity' which presses so hard on others: the male subject must 'sink' (a very Freudian image) his 'femininity' in order to inscribe himself on the side of masculinity. This does not, however, lessen the reader's sense of the savagery with which 'mystic boundaries' are scored (arbitrarily) on the body of the earth/the bodies of female and colonial subjects, in order to maintain the structures of patriarchy and imperialism.

In *Three Guineas* the question which remains open is how to contest the drawing of these mystic boundaries, in relation to gender especially. Some of Woolf's suggestions in this context seem to recall the idealistic, 'difference' feminism of her earlier fiction. For example, she argues from the evidence of memoirs and autobiographies that the 'professional women' of the nineteenth century practised a particular form of negative virtue – 'not to be recognized; not to be egotistical; to do the work for the sake of doing the work'. She quotes from Josephine Butler's description of the women who assisted her in her campaign against child prostitution. Butler wrote that:

The utter absence in them of any desire for recognition, of any vestige of egotism in any form, is worthy of remark. In the purity of their motives they shine out 'clear as crystal'. (*TG*, p. 264)

Woolf suggests that these 'crystalline' women had acquired something in the course of their 'unpaid-for' domestic education which it would be 'extremely foolish' to throw away: in other words she is arguing that there are valuable elements in (culturally constructed) femininity which might form the basis both for contesting the *status quo* and for the creation of new subjectivities/societies in the future. This might remind us of the 'idealistic' feminism of *Jacob's Room* and *Mrs Dalloway*, in particular.

Woolf does not, however, argue that women should *stay* within the 'private' sphere: they should enter education and the professions with a view to transforming them from within. Again, however, we might note that Woolf's suggestions for change are couched in somewhat negative terms. Women's potential input into education, for example, is described in the following way:

> If we are asked to teach, we can examine very carefully into the aim of such teaching, and refuse to teach any art or science that encourages war. Further, we can pour mild scorn upon chapels, upon degrees, and upon the value of examinations ... If we are asked to lecture we can refuse to bolster up the vain and vicious system of lecturing by refusing to lecture. (*TG*, p. 204)

Subversion seems to consist more in the refusal of existing values/institutions than in the positive creation of new ones. Similarly, when Woolf considers the ways in which the professions might be reformed, the emphasis is as much on refusal as on change.

Woolf argues that middle-class women must 'refuse to be separated' from their habitual teachers of 'poverty, chastity, derision and freedom from unreal loyalties': only thus can they enter the professions and yet 'remain civilised human beings'. Woolf defines poverty in rather vague terms as 'enough money to live upon', while chastity consists in the refusal to sell one's mind for money. 'Ridicule, obscurity and censure' ('derision') are, Woolf argues, 'preferable for psychological reasons' to fame and praise. Freedom from unreal loyalties is, finally, defined thus:

> you must rid yourself of pride and nationality in the first place; also, of religious pride, college pride, school pride, family pride, sex pride and those unreal loyalties that spring from them. (*TG*, p. 271)

It could be argued, then, that Woolf's 'feminist' challenge to patriarchy's 'mystic boundaries' consists only of reactive and/or negative responses. These, in Derridean terms, would be seen as simply acting as the 'supplement' of already-existing values. Alternatively, Woolf's 'new', 'resisting' qualities could be seen in Foucauldian terms and viewed as checks and balances produced by a power-system which both includes and exceeds them. Either perspective would suggest that *Three Guineas* could be read as a text which encodes circularity and entrapment. Indeed, Woolf herself draws attention to this element in her text through her repeated allusions to the children's rhyme, 'Here we go round the mulberry bush'. This song takes children ritualistically through their own daily actions ('This is the way we brush our hair', and so on and so on) and is thus well fitted to convey that sense of routine and inevitability which Woolf associates with the 'mulberry tree' or 'sacred tree of property', i.e. with capitalism/patriarchy. So she writes:

> It seems as if there were no progress in the human race, but only repetition. We can almost hear them if we listen singing the same old song, 'Here we go round the mulberry tree, the mulberry tree, the mulberry tree' and if we add, 'of property, of property, of property,' we shall fill in the rhyme without doing violence to the facts. (*TG*, pp. 248–9)

Set against this sense of inevitability is Woolf's argument for the formation of the famous 'Outsiders' Society', which might, she suggests, work for 'justice and equality and liberty for all men and women – outside your society, not within'. Her argument is that a position 'outside' society (and its privileges) might offer a point of leverage, a position from which disinterested criticism might proceed. The objection to this is, of course, that there is no such thing as disinterested criticism *because* there is no place 'outside' society. As was noted above, the work of Derrida and Foucault points to the ways in which critical perspectives are inevitably bound up with that which they contest, and it could be argued that the ambiguous name of the 'Outsiders' Society' reflects exactly this paradox. An 'Outsider's Society' is, of course, a contradiction in terms, a seeming paradox which points to the fact that outside and inside (society) are, in practice, one and the same.

Woolf's interest in *Three Guineas* in the mechanisms of social coercion/control is confirmed by her use of Antigone as the model of 'dissenting woman' in this text. As in *The Years*, Antigone is invoked as an example of one who stands outside the Law, resisting the blandishments of wealth and power. She is aligned by Woolf both with the suffrage campaigners of the past, and with those who were, at the time when the book was written, protesting against the rise of Fascism in Nazi Germany. Similarly, Creon is presented both as a proto-typical patriarch ('While I live, no woman shall rule me' is a line quoted in the text), and as a precursor of contemporary Fascist dictators:

> Creon . . . who held that 'disobedience is the worst of evils', and that 'whomsoever the city may appoint, that man must be obeyed, in little things and great, in just things and unjust' is typical of certain politicians in the past, and of Herr Hitler and Signor Mussolini in the present. (*TG*, p. 395)

Again, then, Woolf is stressing her theme of the interrelations between private and public worlds, and of the connections between patriarchy and Fascism. She also analyses the way in which power works through individuals like Creon who become devoted to it for its own sake, on principle so to speak. Creon identifies himself completely with the operations of the Law: Antigone, on the other hand, tries, in Woolf's words, to distinguish between 'the laws and the Law', between the Law as implacable regulator of patriarchy and her 'private' conscience. Woolf stresses the potential subversiveness of Antigone's refusal of the Law – 'Tis not my nature to join in hating, but in loving.' However, as we have seen in Chapter 5, Antigone's resistance simply leads to her being buried alive. We could hardly have a clearer image of helplessness: Antigone's immolation (a kind of living death) might thus act as a metaphor for the restrictions placed on the individual in the city state.

It can be argued, then, that *Three Guineas* is a text which confronts the pervasive power of Foucault's 'few major strategies' of knowledge and power in the modern state. While some critics have read *Three Guineas* as a text which celebrates women's marginal position,[4] I'd argue that in it Woolf is more pessimistic about the problems of effecting social change. She repeatedly stresses the difficulty of breaking out of the system which contains one. This point is underscored, I think, by her conclusion, which stresses implication with, as much as challenge to, the system:

> Now, since you are pressed for time, let me make an end; apologizing three times over to the three of you, first for the length of this letter, second for the smallness of the contribution, and thirdly for writing at all. The blame for that however rests upon you, *for this letter would never have been written had you not asked for an answer to your own.* (*TG*, p. 367, my italics)

As has been noted, the structure of the text reflects this sense of circularity and impasse. *Three Guineas* takes the form of a perambulation rather than being structured as a purely logical argument. Woolf invents three letters as points of departure (three being a magic number, of course), and then proceeds to enlarge and expand on her arguments, using frequent repetition, or near-repetition. Pamela L. Caughie has argued that Woolf's 'purpose' here is to confound the structures and procedures of patriarchal logic. She suggests that the highly repetitive structure of the text is:

> a highly ironic device that signals the lack of accomplishment and direction that women are accused of by various authorities cited throughout the essay. And it exhausts the argument of the

essay, resisting attempts to reduce it to a progression of logical propositions and undermining any final position, for to impose a position on others would be fascist.[5]

Caughie's argument for Woolf's 'postmodern' refusal of a fixed position in *Three Guineas* is compelling (although it could be objected, of course, that Woolf *is* imposing a relativist position). Caughie argues that the changing viewpoints and methods of *Three Guineas* enable Woolf not to 'find the law' but 'to trace the laws, to find the connections, and to remake them over and over again'.[6]

However, convincing though this argument is, it could also be argued that the pragmatic relativism of *Three Guineas* is shot through with a pessimism which threatens to destabilise the text, to compromise its 'postmodern' composure. An example occurs in Part Two, when Woolf vividly evokes her sense of the impasse facing the feminist of her generation. In philosophical terms, she is faced with the impossibility of breaking out of the mutually reinforcing, restrictive terms of the binary opposition femininity/masculinity. In political terms, her choice is between the restrictions of 'the feminine' and the oppressions of 'the masculine'. Woolf rehearses the arguments and expresses her sense of helplessness in terms which anticipate, uncannily, her subsequent suicide:

we, daughters of educated men, are between the devil and the deep sea. Behind us lies the patriarchal system; the private house, with its nullity, its immorality, its hypocrisy, its servility. Before us lies the public world, the professional system, with its possessiveness, its jealousy, its pugnacity, its greed. The one shuts us up like slaves in a harem; the

other forces us to circle, like caterpillars head to
tail, round and round the mulberry tree, the sacred
tree, of property. It is a choice of evils. Each is bad.
Had we not better plunge off the bridge into the
river; give up the game; declare that the whole of
human life is a mistake and so end it? (*TG*, p. 261)

Woolf's 'outsider position (or as Kristeva might
argue, her 'marginality') offers no more than the
realisation that there is no 'outside', no truly free
space. Particularly, there is no such space in terms of
sex/gender construction. The young child is forced to
choose between the womb (harem) or the phallus
(tree), between reproduction or production (the
industrious silkworm feeds on the mulberry tree):
there is no 'free zone' except in the memory/fantasy of
the pre-Oedipal.

Between the Acts

In *Between the Acts*, Woolf extends the critique of
patriarchy, militarism and imperialism found in *Three
Guineas*. As in so many of her texts, she here traces the
construction of gender identity via the 'Oedipus
complex' (alluded to, of course, in *Three Guineas*). Near
the beginning of *Between the Acts* there is a reworking of
that scene in *To the Lighthouse* in which James suffers
the intervention of his father, disturbing 'the perfect
simplicity and good sense of his relations with his
mother'.[7] George, Isa's small son, has a 'moment of
vision' when he is grubbing about in the flowerbeds
after breakfast:

George grubbed. The flower blazed between the
angles of the roots. Membrane after membrane was

torn. It blazed a soft yellow, a lambent light under a film of velvet; it filled the caverns behind the eyes with light. All that inner darkness became a hall, leaf smelling, earth smelling of yellow light. And the tree was beyond the flower; the grass, the flower and the tree were entire. Down on his knees grubbing he held the flower complete. Then there was a roar and a hot breath and a stream of coarse grey hair rushed between him and the flower. Up he leapt, toppling in his fright, and saw coming towards him a terrible peaked eyeless monster moving on legs, brandishing arms.

'Good morning, sir,' a hollow voice boomed at him from a beak of paper.[8]

While this closely parallels a scene in *Moments of Being* in which Woolf apprehends (in memory) the wholeness and integrity of a flower, it is clear that this moment in *Between the Acts* has been given a further and particular inflection. The flower here signifies not only wholeness but also the mother and/or the female genitalia (we notice the iconography of membranes, halls and caverns). George holds this 'entire' before the interruption from old Bart, his grandfather, who separates him from the mother/the flower by waving the same newspaper in which Isa will later read of a rape carried out by soldiers. Bart could hardly be more representative of the patriarchal forces with which George must now *identify*, on pain of being labelled forever a 'cry-baby' and a coward.

The perpetuation of male dominance is secured through this mechanism of identification, which ensures a continuity between Bart, Giles and George. The dominance of Bart and Giles is particularly stressed in this text: as we shall see, Bart is identified with the power of imperialism, while Giles is almost a

parody of the 'man of action' – after killing the snake/
toad his shoes, we learn, are bloodstained and sticky –
'But it was action. Action relieved him. He strode to
the barn . . .'. By contrast, the women in the text, and
particularly Isa, are passive, though not unaware of
the constraints of their role. Isa is particularly critical
of woman's function as 'sacred vessel', the bearer of
men's children. She resents Bart's feeling that 'She in
her striped dress continued him', and chafes against
the use of her body to continue the male line:

> And she loathed the domestic, the possessive; the
> maternal. And he knew it and did it on purpose to
> tease her, the old brute, her father-in-law. (*BA*,
> p. 17)

The characterisation of Bart as 'the old brute' ties in
with Woolf's emphasis, here as in *Three Guineas*, on the
damaging effect of current gender divisions. Through
the motif, or leitmotif, of the rape of a young girl,
Woolf stresses the dangers of 'masculinity' as it was/is
currently constructed. As Gillian Beer has shown[9], the
rape Isa reads of actually occurred, in April 1938. A
girl of fourteen was lured into the horseguards'
barracks by the 'fantastic' device of asking whether
she would like to see a horse with a green tail, and was
then attacked. The incident, which was reported in
The Times, offered Woolf the opportunity of inserting
into a fictional text a scene which, had it been
invented (with the details of the phallic tail and the
Whitehall/government setting) would indeed have
seemed 'fantastic', exaggerated. It offers an almost
perfect illustration of the thesis developed in *Three
Guineas*: men's upbringing and education encourages
the kind of aggression and assertiveness which,
ultimately, make war inevitable.

However, if Woolf stresses the links between the cult of masculinity and militarism, she also explores in this text the links between the acceptance of 'feminine' identity and war. Lucy Swithin, for example, is identified with the 'feminine' values which have earlier been associated with characters such as Mrs Ramsay. In an exchange centring, as in the earlier text, on the possibility of rain, Lucy contests her brother Bart's bleak view of the world, and calls up the following response from Isa:

> What an angel she was – the old woman! Thus to salute the children; to beat up against those immensities and the old man's irreverences her skinny hands, her laughing eyes! How courageous to defy Bart and the weather! (*BA*, p. 22)

Lucy (born, of course, in the Victorian period) does indeed retain many of the characteristics of the 'Angel' in the house. She harmonises, conciliates, not minding if William Dodge therefore thinks her 'inconsequent, sentimental, foolish'. She is closely identified with the 'feminine' narrative of domesticity, literally telling William the 'story of the house' as she takes him round after lunch:

> 'Then,' said Mrs Swithin, in a low voice, as if the exact moment for speech had come, as if she had promised, and it was time to fulfil her promise, 'come, come and I'll show you the house.' (*BA*, p. 62)

However, Lucy's story/world of reproduction under patriarchy (she takes William from the room where she was born, then to the nursery, and so on) is subjected to critique in this text. Her values are challenged by Giles, at whom she laughs because of his 'job in the city'. On one of the few occasions when we have access to Giles's thoughts, we see that her mockery is unfair, for Giles, with 'no special gift, no capital' had no choice in taking up his profession. And from his standpoint outside the domestic sphere, Giles sees that Lucy, in supporting the values of 'the private house', is as responsible as he is for the threat of imminent war:

> Thus only could he show his irritation, his rage with old fogies who sat and looked at views over coffee and cream . . . At any moment guns would rake that land into furrows; planes splinter Bolney Minster into smithereens and blast the Folly. He, too, loved the view and blamed Aunt Lucy, looking at views, instead of – doing what? What she had done was to marry a squire now dead; she had borne two children, one in Canada, the other, married, in Birmingham. (*BA*, p. 49)

Lucy, as wife and mother, is as complicit as her brother Bart with the (re)production of the society which has brought Europe to the brink of war. Giles's understanding here of the interdependence of public and private spheres is of course close to Woolf's position in *Three Guineas*.

Woolf's critique of imperialism in this text is expressed partly through the characterisation of Bart, whose very name doubles, of course, as an abbreviation for baronet and is thus suggestive of the masculine orders and privileges which Woolf satirises in *Three Guineas*. Bart's dreams of empire are also given a setting which stresses the link between patriarchal patterns of inheritance, militarism, and imperialism. Bart dreams in a chair with his hound at his feet, in a posture which reminds us of the ancestor about whom it is rumoured that he wished his dog 'buried at his feet, in the same grave, about 1750'. Bart's dream also contains elements which remind us of the spiritual stasis and failure explored in *The Waste Land* ('But there is no water', V, 358; '(Come in under the shadow of this red rock)', I, 26):

> But the master was not dead; only dreaming; drowsily, seeing as in a glass, its lustre spotted, himself, a young man helmeted; and a cascade falling. But no water; and the hills, like grey stuff pleated; and in the sand a hoop of ribs; a bullock maggot-eaten in the sun; and in the shadow of the rock, savages; and in his hand a gun. (*BA*, p. 16)

The critique of empire is also presented dramatically through Miss La Trobe's parody of Victorian materialism as embodied in the 'eminent, dominant' Victorian policeman (played in the pageant by the local publican):

> *Purity our watchword; prosperity and respectability. If not, why, let 'em fester in . . .*
> (He paused – no, he had not forgotten his words)
> *Cripplegate; St Giles's; Whitechapel; the Minories. Let 'em sweat at the mines; cough at the looms; rightly endure their lot. That's the price of Empire; that's the white man's burden. And, I can tell you, to direct the traffic orderly, at 'Yde Park Corner, Picadilly Circus, is a whole-time, white man's job. (*BA*, p. 146)*

Miss La Trobe also subverts the conventions of the Empire Day pageant (amongst other things) by turning the mirrors back on the audience at the end of the play, rather than providing them with a story, a version of history, which will reinforce their prejudices and preconceptions. ('Why leave out the British Army? What's history without the Army, eh?' asks Colonel Mayhew, echoing inadvertently, as it were, the question Woolf puts to the reader in *A Room of One's Own* and in *Three Guineas*.)

If Woolf presses some of the questions of *Three Guineas* further in this novel, in her exploration of spiritual sterility and of male sexual violence, for example, she also extends its scope beyond that of her previous fiction by considering in it the parallel between ontogeny and phylogeny, that is, between the history of the individual and the history of the human race. In *Between the Acts*, Woolf moves continually, if lightly, between the prehistory of the individual (pre-Oedipal and pre-linguistic) and the prehistory of the race (that is, before the existence of written records). Woolf's interest in this parallel may have come from her reading of Freud. In *Moses and Monotheism*, which Woolf was reading as she drafted *Between the Acts*, Freud contends that :

> in the history of the human species something happened similar to the events in the life of the individual. That is to say, mankind as a whole also passed through conflicts of a sexual-aggressive nature, which left permanent traces but which were for the most part warded off and forgotten; later, after a long period of latency, they came to life again and created phenomena similar in structure and tendency to neurotic symptoms.[10]

Emphasising the analogy between the life of the individual and that of the race, Freud also suggests that just as the adult retains memories from his own childhood experience, so he retains too 'memory-traces of the experiences of former generations'. The celebrated 'orts, scraps and fragments' of *Between the Acts* are perhaps intended to carry something of the resonance of what Freud called 'fragments of phylogenetic origin, an archaic heritage'.[11]

Although the influence of Freud is marked in *Between the Acts*, Woolf modifies the model of evolutionary development which Freud had taken from Darwin. As Gillian Beer has argued,[12] Woolf 'tempers the triumphalist narrative of development' associated with Darwin, stressing instead the continuity between the prehistoric and the present. Woolf calls into question an evolutionary narrative which would downgrade the experience of so-called 'savages' or 'primitives', and in one passage has Isa's dentist (a semi-comic representative of modern barbarism) impressing on her the medical and scientific skills of so-called primitive peoples:

> 'Once there was no sea,' said Mrs Swithin. 'No sea at all between us and the continent. I was reading that in a book this morning. There were rhododendrons in the Strand; and mammoths in Picadilly.'
> 'When we were savages,' said Isa.
> Then she remembered; her dentist had told her that savages could perform very skilful operations on the brain. Savages had false teeth, he said. False teeth were invented, she thought he said, in the time of the Pharaohs. (*BA*, p. 27)

Woolf's resistance to the developmental evolutionary plot can thus be linked not only with her distrust of 'the causal forms she associates with nineteenth century narratives', as Beer suggests, but also with that critique of imperialism, with its assumption of a contrast between 'primitive' and 'developed' peoples, which animates this text and *Three Guineas*.

To turn back once more to *Moses and Monotheism*, it is worth pointing out a further connection between Woolf's text and Freud's. (It is also worth registering here the possible connections between Woolf's *Three Guineas* and Freud's *Group Psychology and the Analysis of the Ego*, which Woolf was reading in the 'thirties.) In *Moses and Monotheism*, Freud offers in his 'primal horde' theory (developed from an hypothesis of Darwin) an account of the origins of patriarchy which Woolf might have found suggestive, with its emphasis on the despotic older male appropriating all the females in his 'horde' and disposing of younger, competing males. Freud's account emphasises, of course, parallels between this (his)story and the 'family romance' which he had outlined in the *Three Essays on Sexuality*. Freud then explores a range of cultural myths about 'the hero', who represents, in his view, the younger man who supplants the patriarch and/or the son in the family romance. In all such myths, Freud argues, the same elements are present: the hero is the son of parents of the highest station; he is born against his father's will; he is ordered to be killed, but survives, being placed in most cases 'in a casket and delivered to the waves'; he is nurtured by animals or poor people and eventually grows up to enter into his inheritance and supplant his father.

In *Between the Acts*, Woolf reworks this archetypal story, which relates both to the history of the individual and the history of the race. It first appears in the 'Elizabethan' play within a play:

> About a false duke; and a Princess disguised as a boy; then the long lost heir turns out to be the beggar, because of a mole on his cheek; and Carinthia – that's the Duke's daughter, only she's been lost in a cave – falls in love with Ferdinando

who had been put into a basket as a baby by an aged crone. And they marry. (*BA*, p. 80)

Through this scrambling together of motifs from Elizabethan and Jacobean drama (especially Shakespeare's last plays), Woolf demonstrates the pervasiveness of the myths which, without our necessarily being aware of it, reflect but also reinforce the structures of patriarchy in our culture. Elizabethan drama is rich in examples (compare the 'deep structure' of Webster's plays, for example, one of which is alluded to in Miss La Trobe's play). In the Restoration period (which was, it could be argued, one of greater cultural freedom) something of a reversal took place. To a limited extent, counter-myths could be produced by women writers such as Aphra Behn who had gained economic independence through writing. In *Between the Acts*, then, it is not surprising to find that in Miss La Trobe's second, Restoration play, the Moses myth is rewritten *as if by a woman*, and the baby found in a basket is a girl, whose inheritance (i.e. financial independence) gives the play its title, *Where there's a Will there's a Way*. The play scenes in the pageant thus reflect (on) the relationship between dominant cultural myths and the (usually muted) position of women writers. Woolf could almost be retelling here the story of women's cultural production also told in *A Room of One's Own*. The 'story' ends here with the incarceration of 'woman' in the Victorian period: in the third play we watch Evelyn Harcastle making the mistake that Jane Eyre did not make, following a St John Rivers-like figure – an emblem of patriarchal imperialism – to convert the heathen in Africa. By then turning what would have been a fourth play into Miss La Trobe's fragmented mirrors Woolf suggests, of course, that the story in the traditional sense (the story of

English literature/culture) is over, in part because of
the changes which have come about in the relationship of the author (of either sex) to the audience; in
part also, however, because of changing conceptions of
gender.

Between the Acts thus explores the relations between
the individual and the wider historical plot in/of
patriarchy. Through the pageant, in particular, Woolf
refers to stories and histories about the 'development'
of the human race; in the rest of the text she
concentrates on the history of the individual (for
example, showing us George at the moment of
Oedipal crisis). However, what interests Woolf still
more in this text is that which comes before either race
or individual history, that which comes, indeed, before
prehistory. Restlessly in *Between the Acts*, Woolf works
at the question of origins. In a famous passage, Lucy
Swithin imagines a time when the planet was popu-
lated by dinosaurs, and literally then thinks the
unthinkable, merging animal and human in a figure
half 'grace' and half monster:

> It took her five seconds in actual time, in mind
> time ever so much longer, to separate Grace herself,
> with blue china on a tray, from the leather-covered
> gruntling monster who was about, as the door
> opened, to demolish a whole tree in the green
> steaming undergrowth of the primeval forest. (*BA*,
> p. 8)

Our animal 'origins' are almost impossible to conceive,
but Woolf continually reminds us in this text of the
origins of the human race (according to evolutionary
theory) in amphibian or crustacean life-forms. In one
passage, for example, Woolf deftly establishes the
parallel between the origins of (individual) human life

in the amniotic fluid of the maternal body, and the origins of the human race in the sea. Lucy and Bart are thinking of their childhood by the sea, then the perspective shifts to Isa's view of herself as mother:

> 'You can't expect it brought to your door in a pail of water,' said Mrs Swithin, 'as I remember when we were children, living in a house by the sea. Lobsters, fresh from the lobster pots. How they pinched the stick cook gave them! . . .'
> . . . They were bringing up nets full of fish from the sea; but Isa was seeing – the garden, variable as the forecast said, in the light breeze. Again, the children passed and she tapped on the window and blew them a kiss. In the drone of the garden it went unheeded. (*BA*, pp. 26–7)

The comic play, in the first part of the book, on the condition and status of the fish for lunch (fresh or 'whiffy'?) is clearly related to this theme, the fish being a link between 'ourselves' and our aquatic ancestors.

In relation to the origins of the individual, Woolf offers in *Between the Acts* a parodic version of that 'primal scene' which is so closely woven in with her meditations on the origin of writing in *A Room of One's Own* and 'A Sketch of the Past'. As she takes William Dodge around the house, Lucy Swithin cautiously approaches her (long-dead) parents' room:

> 'Now,' she said, 'for the bedrooms.' She tapped twice very distinctly on a door. With her head on one side, she listened.
> 'One never knows', she murmured, 'if there's somebody there.' Then she flung open the door.
> He half expected to see somebody there, naked,

or half dressed, or knelt in prayer. But the room was empty. The room was tidy as a pin, not slept in for months, a spare room. (*BA*, p. 64)

Although Lucy tiptoes up to the room like the child she once was, the room of origin (she was born in this room) is now void of significance: it has become simply a 'spare' room. However, the question of individual human origins is broached with renewed intensity in Miss La Trobe's final vision, which anticipates the last lines of the text:

'I should group them', she murmured, 'here.' It would be midnight; there would be two figures, half concealed by a rock. The curtain would rise. What would the first words be? (*BA*, p. 189)

The house had lost its shelter. It was night before roads were made, or houses. It was the night that dwellers in caves had watched from some high place among rocks.
    Then the curtain rose. They spoke. (*BA*, p. 197)

What is the significance of Woolf's preoccupation with origins in *Between the Acts*? Could it be that these images of origin in fact offer a way of thinking about/ imagining the future? It could be argued that Woolf's concentration on cycles of creation, growth and decay in *Between the Acts* helped to create a perspective within which she could think about what might happen *after* the war – a war which she viewed as the result of patriarchal, capitalist human development. Such a future might be seen as post-humanist and post-individualist, and I'd argue that it is this *future* that Woolf is moving towards when she envisages a time 'before time was':

Empty, empty, empty; silent, silent, silent. The room was a shell, singing of what was before time was; a vase stood in the heart of the house, alabaster, smooth, cold, holding the still, distilled essence of emptiness, silence. (*BA*, pp. 33–4)

This quotation is reminiscent of an early account of the project of *The Waves*. In the first draft of that novel, Woolf wrote:

I am trying to find in the folds of the past such fragments as time preserves . . . there was a napkin, a flowerpot and a book. I am telling the story of the world from the beginning, and in a small room, whose windows are open.[13]

In both passages (and to an extent in both novels), Woolf is trying to suggest the unimaginable, a time before or outside human consciousness. She is reaching back to stillness, emptiness, a time before human subjectivity. This project is linked both with Woolf's attempt in *The Waves* to describe a 'world without a self' and with Isa's experience of an I-less/eyeless world in *Between the Acts*:

'Where do I wander?' she mused. 'Down what draughty tunnels? Where the eyeless wind blows? And there grows nothing for the eye. No rose. To issue where? In some harvestless dim field where no evening lets fall her mantle; nor sun rises. All's equal there.' (*BA*, pp. 138–9)

The imaginative recreation of a world without a self not only points back to a time before human history, but can also point forward to a post-individualist, post-humanist future. It is surely such a future which the text moves towards through such devices as Miss La Trobe's famously 'unfair' attack on her audience at the end of the pageant:

> Out they leapt, jerked, skipped. Flashing, dazzling, dancing, jumping. Now old Bart . . . he was caught. Now Manresa. Here a nose . . . There a skirt . . . Then trousers only . . . Now perhaps a face . . . Ourselves? But that's cruel. To snap us as we are, before we've had time to assume . . . And only, too, in parts . . . That's what's so distorting and upsetting and utterly unfair. (*BA*, p. 165)

This 'unfair' attack might be read as an attack on the illusion of the existence of the transcendental human subject. It could be argued that Miss La Trobe's mirrors reflect the incoherence and discontinuity of what we think of as 'ourselves', before we have had time to 'assume' (in both senses) a unified self. It is as though these mirrors undo the work of the Lacanian mirror stage in which, according to Lacan, the child first *imagines* itself as a whole entity. The mirrors destroy the illusion of the unity of the self which has underpinned Western (humanist) thought from the time of the Renaissance (the time at which Miss La Trobe's pageant begins) to 'the present time'. The audience in *Between the Acts* is thus forced to see the body/self in pieces, to recognise that 'we' consist merely of 'orts, scraps and fragments'.

Only Mrs Manresa, identified expressly with humanism, or with 'the jolly human heart' retains the illusion of self in front of the mirrors, adding a mirror of her own in order, narcissistically, to 'touch up' her appearance. The rest of the audience watches the disintegration of the 'characters' from the play, who, mirroring the audience, put off a coherent identity and simply repeat arbitrary fragments of their parts:

I am not (said one) *in my perfect mind . . . Another, Reason am I . . . And I? I'm the old top hat . . . Home is the hunter, home from the hill . . . Home? Where the miner sweats, and the maiden faith is rudely strumpeted . . . Sweet and low; sweet and low, wind of the western sea . . . Is that a dagger that I see before me? . . . The owl hoots and the ivy mocks tap-tap-tapping on the pane . . . Lady I love till I die, leave thy chamber and come . . . Where the worm weaves its winding sheet . . . (BA, p. 166)*

At the very end of the play, Woolf/La Trobe seems to modify this sense of fragmentation and disunity, as a record is put on which both harmonises and humanises – it is characterised as '*somebody* speaking after the anonymous bray of the infernal megaphone' (my italics). The music suggests unity in/beneath disunity:

Not the melody of surface sound alone controlled it; but also the warring battle-plumed warriors straining asunder: To part? No. Compelled from the ends of the horizon; recalled from the edge of appalling crevasses; they crashed; solved; united. (*BA*, p. 170)

Any optimistic investment in music as an image of harmony (in the self and in the community) is rather undercut, however, as the music heard by Mr Streatfield a few moments later turns out to come from (fighter?) planes flying overhead in formation – '*That* was the music'.

It could be argued, then, that Woolf is extremely sceptical in this text about the unity of the self (and indeed about the unity achieved by art). Indeed, it could be suggested that in *Between the Acts* Woolf anticipates much with which we have become familiar in postmodern thought and culture. In particular, there is a strong sense in *Between the Acts* of the

breakdown of monolithic concepts of identity, underpinned by fixed gender categories. Instead, Woolf
prefers to note the multiplicity of the self, writing of
the 'population' of the mind. In relation to such a
'death of the subject', Woolf's text is, however,
marked by a certain optimism. If humanism and
individualism have brought us to the verge of war,
perhaps a post-individualist, post-humanist consciousness might offer improved possibilities for
the future. The notion of constantly shifting alignments of *dispersed* subjectivities offers, perhaps, a more
appropriate model for continued human existence
than conceptions of self and society revolving round
the idea(l) of the transcendent subject. Certainly
feminists have been quick to see that such 'dispersal'
might have a good deal to recommend it. Judith
Butler, for example, has recently argued the case for a
fluid, 'coalitional' gender politics:

> An open coalition, then, will affirm identities that
> are alternately instituted and relinquished accord-
> ing to the purposes at hand; it will be an open
> assemblage that permits of multiple convergences
> and divergences without obedience to a normative
> telos of definitional closure.[14]

If one effect of Miss La Trobe's mirrors is to show us
the 'subject in pieces', a second and related effect is
the calling into question of the rigid border between
human and animal existence (this is also, incidentally,
a point stressed by Freud in *Moses and Monotheism*).
The mirrors create a fragmentation and chaos which
extends into and becomes continuous with that of the
animal world:

> Mopping, mowing, whisking, frisking, the look-
> ing glasses darted, flashed, exposed. People in the

back rows stood up to see the fun. Down they sat,
caught themselves ... What an awful show-up!
Even for the old who, one might suppose, hadn't
any longer any care about their faces ... And Lord!
the jangle and the din! The very cows joined in.
Walloping, tail lashing, the reticence of nature was
undone, and the barriers which should divide Man
the Master from the Brute were dissolved. (*BA*,
p. 165)

Again, this aspect of *Between the Acts* seems to point to
the possibility of imagining a post-humanist future, of
imagining 'life' continuing after the war, but not
necessarily in the strictly human/humanist terms in
which we are used to conceiving of it. Such a view
might be supported by a reading of the passage in
which Miss La Trobe, after the pageant is over,
watches a tree being attacked by starlings:

Then suddenly the starlings attacked the tree
behind which she had hidden. In one flock they
pelted it like so many winged stones. The whole tree
hummed with the whizz they made, as if each bird
plucked a wire. A whizz, a buzz rose from the bird-
buzzing, bird-vibrant, bird-blackened tree. The
tree became a rhapsody, a quivering cacophony, a
whizz and vibrant rapture, branches, leaves, birds
syllabling discordantly life, life, life, without
measure, without stop devouring the tree. (*BA*,
pp. 188–9)

This is one of the most striking scenes in the novel. In
it, it could be argued, the tree operates as an image for
the Tree of Man (rather like the 'mulberry tree' of
patriarchy/capitalism in *Three Guineas*, which, Woolf
suggests, should also be 'pelted', with laughter and

destroyed). In *Between the Acts*, this tree seems to be undone and transformed by the explosion of an animal life which changes its monolithic singleness into a new, 'quivering' and 'discordant' 'life, life, life'.[15] Animal life modulates into and modifies human life, as it does in Miss La Trobe's final vision, which brings the animal and human creatively together:

> There was the high ground at midnight; there the rock; and two scarcely perceptible figures. Suddenly the tree was pelted by starlings. She set down her glass. She heard the first words. (*BA*, p. 191)

In this blurring of the boundaries between animal and human, Woolf again seems to anticipate aspects of post-humanist or postmodernist thought. We might, for example, set Woolf's vision in *Between the Acts* alongside Donna Haraway's articulation of similar insights in her 1985 'Manifesto for Cyborgs':

> Nothing really convincingly settles the separation of human and animal. Many people no longer feel the need of such a separation; indeed, many branches of feminist culture affirm the pleasure of connection with human and other living creatures . . . Biology and evolutionary theory over the last two centuries have simultaneously produced modern organisms as objects of knowledge and reduced the line between humans and animals to a faint trace.[16]

It is, perhaps, in such a context of the vivid imagination of the new, and of the possibilities of a post-individualist and post-humanist future, that we should place the final 'putting out of the light' of the individual human subject, Virginia Woolf, in March 1941.

Notes

The edition of Woolf's novels referred to throughout is The World's Classics edition (Oxford: Oxford University Press, 1992).

Preface

1. See Jane Marcus (ed.), *New Feminist Essays on Virginia Woolf* (London: Macmillan, 1981); *Virginia Woolf and the Languages of Patriarchy* (Bloomington: Indiana University Press, 1987).

2. Daniel Ferrer, *Virginia Woolf and the Madness of Language*, trans. Geoffrey Bennington and Rachel Bowlby (London: Routledge, 1990).

3. See *Jacques Lacan and the école freudienne. Feminine Sexuality*, ed. Juliet Mitchell and Jacqueline Rose (London: Macmillan, 1982), p. 49 for further discussion of this point.

4. Margaret Whitford, 'The Feminist Philosopher: A Contradiction in Terms?', *Women*, 3, 2 (Autumn 1992), 117–18.

Chapter 1: Introduction

1. See, for example, Quentin Bell, *Virginia Woolf: A Biography* (London: Hogarth Press, 1972, 2 vols; repr. Triad/Paladin, 1976); Leonard Woolf, *Downhill All the Way: An Autobiography of the Years 1919 to 1939* (London: Hogarth Press, 1967).

2. Virginia Woolf quoted in Lyndall Gordon, *Virginia Woolf: A Writer's Life* (Oxford: Oxford University Press, 1984), p. 6.

3. See Bell, *Virginia Woolf*, I, 18–20.

4. Virginia Woolf, *Moments of Being*, ed. with an introduction by Jeanne Schulkind (London: Grafton Books, 1989), p. 128. All subsequent references will be incorporated into the text.

5. Virginia Woolf, *A Writer's Diary* (London: Hogarth Press, 1953), p. 175.

6. Virginia Woolf, 'Professions for Women', in *Women and Writing*, ed. Michèle Barrett (London: Women's Press, 1979), p. 59.

7. See the second part of this chapter for a discussion of female *jouissance*, a French word with no exact equivalent in English, used in psychoanalytic theory to suggest extreme pleasure or (sexual) bliss.

8. Louise DeSalvo, *Virginia Woolf: The Impact of Childhood Sexual Abuse on her Life and Work* (London: Women's Press, 1989), pp. 114–16.

9. Hélène Cixous, *Reading with Clarice Lispector*, trans. and ed. Verena Andermatt Conley (Hemel Hempstead: Harvester Wheatsheaf, 1990), p. 40.

10. DeSalvo, p. 87.

11. Bell, I, 43.

12. DeSalvo, p. 119.

13. Nigel Nicholson and Joanne Trautmann (eds), *The Letters of Virginia Woolf* (6 vols, London: Chatto and Windus, 1975–80), VI, 367–8.

14. Sue Roe, *Writing and Gender: Virginia Woolf's Writing Practice* (Hemel Hempstead: Harvester Wheatsheaf, 1990), p. 174.

15. *Mrs Dalloway*, pp. 45–6.

16. Catherine Stimpson, *Where the Meanings Are* (London: Routledge, 1988), p. 100.

17. See Mary Jacobus, ' "The Third Stroke": Reading Woolf with Freud', in *Grafts: Feminist Cultural Criticism*, ed. Susan Sheridan (London: Verso, 1988), p. 95.

18. *To the Lighthouse*, pp. 88–9.

19. Hélène Cixous and Catherine Clément, *The Newly Born Woman*, trans. Betsy Wing (Manchester: Manchester University Press, 1986), p. 85.

20. Ibid., pp. 90–1.

21. Ibid., pp. 91–2.

22. Elaine Showalter, *A Literature of Their Own* (London: Virago, 1978), p. 267.

23. Stephen Trombley, *'All that Summer She Was Mad': Virginia Woolf and Her Doctors* (London: Junction Books, 1981), p. 2.

24. DeSalvo, xvi.

25. Ibid., p. 127.

26. Toril Moi (ed.), *The Kristeva Reader* (Oxford: Blackwell, 1986), p. 157. As Makiko Minow-Pinkney suggests, Kristeva here refers to 'Miss Brown' instead of 'Miss Bowen' (Elizabeth Bowen).

27. Ferrer, p. 7.

28. *A Room of One's Own; Three Guineas*, p. 136.

29. Rosi Braidotti, *Patterns of Dissonance* (Cambridge: Polity Press, 1991) p. 228.

30. Fouque, quoted in Braidotti, p. 227.

31. Fouque in Elaine Marks and Isabelle de Courtivron (eds), *New French Feminisms* (Brighton: Harvester, 1981), p. 118.

32. *Mrs Dalloway*, p. 165.

33. *To the Lighthouse*, p. 70.

Chapter 2: Moving Out

1. *The Voyage Out*, p. 87. All subsequent references will be incorporated into the text.

2. Alice Fox, *Virginia Woolf and the Literature of the English Renaissance* (Oxford: Clarendon Press, 1990), pp. 22–3.

3. Annette Kolodny, *The Lay of the Land: Metaphor as Experience and History in American Life and Letters* (Chapel Hill: University of North Carolina Press, 1975).

4. John Berryman, 'Conrad's Journey', in *The Freedom of the Poet* (New York: Farrar, Strauss and Giroux, 1976), pp. 110–11.

5. Avril Horner and Sue Zlosnik, *Landscapes of Desire* (Hemel Hempstead: Harvester Wheatsheaf, 1990), pp. 83–4.

6. Anne Olivier Bell and Andrew McNeillie (eds), *The Diary of Virginia Woolf*, 5 vols (London: Hogarth Press, 1977–84), II, 17.

7. *Moments of Being*, p. 156.

8. *Jacob's Room*, p. 89. Subsequent references will be incorporated into the text.

9. *A Room of One's Own; Three Guineas*, p. 62.

10. Makiko Minow-Pinkney, *Virginia Woolf and the Problem of the Subject* (Brighton: Harvester Press, 1987).

11. Rachel Bowlby, *Virginia Woolf: Feminist Destinations* (Oxford: Blackwell, 1988), p. 112.

12. In this connexion, see Kate Flint's article 'Revising *Jacob's Room*: Virginia Woolf, Women and Language', *The Review of English Studies*, XLII, 167 (August 1991), 361–79. Flint demonstrates that Woolf deleted material relating to the bodily lives of women when revising the text. Flint argues that this shows Woolf's awareness of the need to acknowledge dominant cultural codes in order to intervene successfully in sexual politics. Equally, however, it suggests the *primacy* of the maternal/bodily for Woolf.

13. See Minow-Pinkney, p. 30.

14. See Bowlby, p. 103.

15. See Gayatri Spivak, 'Unmaking and Making in *To the Lighthouse*', in *In Other Worlds: Essays in Cultural Politics* (London: Methuen, 1987).

16. Jacobus, p. 106.

Chapter 3: Romancing the Feminine

1. *Mrs Dalloway*, p. 16. All subsequent references will be incorporated into the text.

2. Ferrer, p. 24.

3. Minow-Pinkney, p. 80.

4. Virginia Woolf, *Women and Writing*, ed. Michèle Barrett, p. 191.

5. Sue Roe, *Writing and Gender*, pp. 172–3.

6. See Horner and Zlosnik, p. 99.

7. Marianne Hirsch, *The Mother/Daughter Plot: Narrative, Psychoanalysis, Feminism* (Bloomington and Indianapolis: Indiana University Press, 1989), p. 96.

8. See Christine Battersby, *Gender and Genius* (London: Women's Press, 1989) for a discussion of earlier manifestations of this tendency.

9. Melanie Klein, *Envy and Gratitude and other works 1946–1963* (London: Virago, 1988), pp. 201–2.

10. Melanie Klein, 'Infantile Anxiety-Situations Reflected in a Work of Art and in the Creative Impulse', repr. in *Love, Guilt and Reparation and other works 1921–1945* (London: Virago, 1988), p. 210–18.

11. Ibid., p. 217.

12. Ibid., p. 218

13. Vanessa Bell quoted in Bell, II, 128.

14. Melanie Klein, 'The Oedipus Complex in the Light of Early Anxieties', repr. in *Love, Guilt and Reparation*, pp. 370–419.

15. *To the Lighthouse*, p. 52. All subsequent references will be incorporated into the text.

16. Jacobus, pp. 103–4.

17. Klein, *Love, Guilt and Reparation*, p. 418.

18. Ibid., p. 354.

19. *The Diary of Virginia Woolf*, III, 34.

20. Klein, *Envy and Gratitude*, p. 141 ('On Identification').

21. Ibid., p. 180 ('Envy and Gratitude').

22. See Chapter 4 for further discussion of Irigaray in this respect.

23. See Spivak, *In Other Worlds*, p. 40.

24. Jacobus, pp. 93–4.

25. Marianne Hirsch, *The Mother/Daughter Plot*, p. 114.

Chapter 4: Imaginary Lives

1. Sherron E. Knopp, ' "If I saw you would you kiss me?" Sapphism and the subversiveness of Virginia Woolf's *Orlando*', repr. in Joseph Bristow (ed.), *Sexual Sameness: Textual Differences in Lesbian and Gay Writing* (London: Routledge, 1992), p. 111.

2. *Letters*, III, 428–9 (my italics).

3. *Orlando*, pp. 34–5. All subsequent references will be incorporated into the text.

4. *A Writer's Diary*, pp. 154–9.

5. See Elaine Showalter, *A Literature of Their Own*, pp. 284–5; Sandra M. Gilbert, 'Costumes of the Mind: Transvesticism and Metaphor in Modern Literature' in Elizabeth Abel (ed.), *Writing and Sexual Difference* (Brighton: Harvester Press, 1982); Gillian Beer, 'The Body of the People in Virginia Woolf' in Sue Roe (ed.), *Women Reading Women's Writing* (Brighton: Harvester Press, 1987).

6. The Pelican Freud Library, vol. 7 (London: Penguin Books Ltd, 1977, repr. 1987), p. 57.

7. Francette Pacteau, 'The Impossible Referent: Representations of the Androgyne' in *Formations of Fantasy*, ed. Victor Burgin, James Donald and Cora Kaplan (London: Methuen, 1986).

8. *A Writer's Diary*, p. 154.

9. See Sue Roe (ed.), *Women Reading Women's Writing*, p. 100.

10. The Pelican Freud Library, vol. 7, p. 376.

11. Adrienne Rich, *Blood, Bread and Poetry: Selected Prose 1979–1985* (London: Virago, 1987), p. 35.

12. Bell, II, 118.

13. *Letters*, III, 381.

14. *A Room of One's Own; Three Guineas*, p. 5. All subsequent references will be incorporated into the text.

15. In connexion with this see Madeline Moore, 'Some Female Versions of Pastoral: *The Voyage Out* and Matriarchal Mythologies' in Jane Marcus (ed.), *New Feminist Essays on Virginia Woolf*, pp. 88–9.

16. *A Writers' Diary*, p. 187.

17. The Pelican Freud Library, vol. 7, p. 376.

18. Quoted in Diane Hamer, 'Significant Others: Lesbians and Psycho-analytic Theory', *Feminist Review*, 34 (Spring 1990), 145.

19. Margaret Whitford, *Luce Irigaray: Philosophy in the Feminine* (London: Routledge, 1991), p. 45.

20. Luce Irigaray, *Speculum of the Other Woman*, trans. Gillian C. Gill (Ithica: Cornell University Press, 1985), p. 210.

21. Whitford, p. 45.

22. Quoted and trans. in Whitford, p. 45.

23. Jane Marcus, 'Sapphistory: the Woolf and the Well' in *Lesbian Texts and Contexts: Radical Revisions*, ed. Karla Jay and Joanne Glasgow (New York: New York University Press, 1990), p. 174.

24. Virginia Woolf, *Women and Fiction: The Manuscript Versions of 'A Room of One's Own'*, transcribed and edited by S. P. Rosenbaum. Shakespeare Head Press (Oxford: Blackwell, 1992).

25. See for example Hamer, cited above.

26. Showalter, *A Literature of Their Own*, p. 289.

27. Sue Roe, *Writing and Gender*, p. 83.

28. Bowlby, pp. 43–4.

Chapter 5: Generation(s)

1. *The Waves*, pp. 3–4. All subsequent references will be incorporated into the text.

2. J. W. Graham (ed.), *The Waves: The Two Holograph Drafts* (London; Hogarth Press, 1976), pp. 63–4.

3. The Pelican Freud Library, vol. 4, p. 524.

4. Graham, p. 7. It should be noted in connexion with this point that the significance of the metaphor of the waves also lies in the fact that, in evolutionary terms, human life had its origins on the sea shore. The waves thus figure not only individual birth, but also the birth/evolution of the human race.

5. See Minow-Pinkney, p. 169.

6. The Pelican Freud, vol. 4, p. 526.

7. Ibid., p. 526.

8. Elizabeth Bronfen, 'From Omphalos to Phallus: Cultural Representations of Femininity and Death', *Women*, 3, 2 (Autumn 1992), 156.

9. Graham, p. 62.

10. *The Letters and Journals of Katherine Mansfield* (Harmondsworth, Penguin Books, 1977), p. 150.

11. *A Writer's Diary*, p. 133.

12. Ibid., p. 211.

13. Hélène Cixous, *Reading with Clarice Lispector*, p. 151.

14. *A Writer's Diary*, p. 180.

15. Graham, p. 6; p. 39.

16. Julia Kristeva, *Powers of Horror: An Essay on Abjection*, trans. Leon S. Roudiez (New York: Columbia University Press, 1982), pp. 34–5.

17. Ibid, p. 38.

18. Gillian Beer, 'Introduction' to *The Waves*, p. xxxvi.

19. Katherine Mansfield, *Collected Stories* (London: Constable, 1945, repr. 1976), p. 205.

20. Françoise Defromont, 'Impossible Mourning' in Paulette Michel and Michel Dupuis (eds), *The Fine Instrument* (Sydney: Dangaroo Press, 1989).

21. *Letters*, VI, 116.

22. Mitchell A. Leaska (ed.), *The Pargiters by Virginia Woolf: The Novel-Essay Portion of 'The Years'* (London: Hogarth Press, 1978), p. vii.

23. Quoted in Patricia Waugh (ed.), *Postmodernism: A Reader* (London: Edward Arnold, 1992), p. 185.

24. Alan Wilde, *Horizons of Assent: Modernism, Postmodernism and the Ironic Imagination* (London: Johns Hopkins University Press, 1981).

25. *Letters*, VI, 115–16.

26. Michel Foucault, *The History of Sexuality*, vol. 1 (London: Penguin Books, 1990), p. 100.

27. Mitchell A. Leaska, *The Pargiters*, pp. 36–7. All subsequent references will be incorporated into the text.

28. *The Years*, p. 154. Subsequent references will be incorporated into the text.

29. Sigmund Freud, 'Analysis Terminable and Interminable' (1937) in *The Standard Edition of the Complete Psychological Works of Sigmund Freud*, XXIII (London: Hogarth Press, 1964).

30. See Susan Squier, 'The Politics of City Space in *The Years*: Street Love, Pillar Boxes and Bridges' in Marcus (ed.), *New Feminist Essays on Virginia Woolf*, pp. 216–37.

31. See *The Pargiters*, p. xxx.

32. Julia Kristeva, 'Women's Time' in Catherine Belsey and Jane Moore (eds), *The Feminist Reader* (London: Macmillan, 1989), p. 215.

33. Hélène Cixous, *The Newly Born Woman*, p.79.

Chapter 6: Coins and Mirrors

1. *A Room of One's Own; Three Guineas*, p. 412 (notes to Part 3). All subsequent references will be incorporated into the text.

2. *The Diary of Virginia Woolf*, IV, 6.

3. The Pelican Freud Library, vol. 7, p. 336.

4. See for example Patricia Waugh in *Feminine Fictions: Revisiting the Postmodern* (London: Routledge, 1989), pp. 92–3.

5. Pamela L. Caughie, *Virginia Woolf and Postmodernism: Literature in Quest and Question of Itself* (Urbana: University of Illinois Press, 1991), p. 116.

6. Ibid., p. 137.

7. *To the Lighthouse*, p. 51.

8. *Between the Acts*, pp.10–11. Subsequent references will be incorporated into the text.

9. See Gillian Beer, 'Introduction' to the Penguin edition of *Between the Acts*, p. xxxiii.

10. Sigmund Freud, *Moses and Monotheism*, trans. Katherine Jones (London: Hogarth Press, 1932), p. 129.

11. Ibid., p. 157.

12. Gillian Beer, 'Virginia Woolf and Pre-History' in Eric Warner (ed.), *Virginia Woolf: A Centenary Perspective* (London: Macmillan, 1984), p. 104.

13. Graham, p. 42.

14. Judith Butler, *Gender Trouble: Feminism and the Subversion of Identity* (London: Routledge, 1990), p. 16.

15. As Mitchell A. Leaska notes in his introduction to *The Letters of Vita Sackville-West to Virginia Woolf*, ed. Louise DeSalvo and Mitchell A. Leaska, 'life, life, life' translates into Latin as 'vita, vita, vita': Woolf exploits this allusive possibility in *Orlando*, too.

16. Donna Haraway, 'A Manifesto for Cyborgs: Science, Technology, and Socialist Feminism in the 1980s' in Linda J. Nicholson (ed.), *Feminism/ Postmodernism* (New York: Routledge, 1990), p. 193.

Bibliography

Works by Virginia Woolf

Fiction

Note: Virginia Woolf's works came out of copyright in 1991. Accordingly, a variety of new editions of her novels have recently become available. For simplicity's sake, details of the first publication only are given below.

The Voyage Out (London: Duckworth, 1915)
Night and Day (London: Duckworth, 1919)
Jacob's Room (London: Hogarth Press, 1922)
Mrs Dalloway (London: Hogarth Press, 1925)
To the Lighthouse (London: Hogarth Press, 1927)
Orlando (London: Hogarth Press, 1928)
The Waves (London: Hogarth Press, 1931)
The Years (London: Hogarth Press, 1937)
Between the Acts (London: Hogarth Press, 1941)
A Haunted House and Other Stories (London: Hogarth Press, 1944).
The Complete Shorter Fiction of Virginia Woolf, ed. Susan Dick (London: Hogarth Press, 1985)

Other Works

Flush: A Biography (London: Hogarth Press, 1933)
Roger Fry (London: Hogarth Press, 1940)
A Room of One's Own (London: Hogarth Press, 1929)
Three Guineas (London: Hogarth Press, 1938)
Collected Essays, ed. Leonard Woolf, 4 vols (London: Chatto and Windus, 1966, 1967)

Autobiographical and Other Writings

Bell, Anne Olivier and Andrew McNeillie (eds), *The Diary of Virginia Woolf*, 5 vols (London: Hogarth Press, 1977–84)

McNeillie, Andrew (ed.), *The Essays of Virginia Woolf*, 6 vols (London: The Hogarth Press, 1986–)

Nicholson, Nigel and Joanne Trautmann (eds), *The Letters of Virginia Woolf*, 6 vols (London: Chatto and Windus, 1975–80)

Woolf, Leonard (ed.), *A Writer's Diary* (London: Hogarth Press, 1953)

Woolf, Virginia, *Moments of Being: Unpublished autobiographical writings*, ed. Joanne Schulkind (revised edn, London: Hogarth Press, 1985)

Editions of Manuscript Drafts

Dick, Susan (ed.), *To the Lighthouse: The Original Holograph Draft* (London: Hogarth Press, 1983)

Graham, J. W. (ed.), *The Waves: The Two Holograph Drafts* (London: Hogarth Press, 1976)

Leaska, Mitchell A. (ed.), *The Pargiters by Virginia Woolf: The Novel-Essay Portion of 'The Years'* (London: Hogarth Press, 1978)

Rosenbaum, S. P. (ed.) *Women and Fiction: The Manuscript Versions of 'A Room of One's Own'* (Oxford: Blackwell, 1992)

Biography

Bell, Quentin, *Virginia Woolf: A Biography*, 2 vols (London: Hogarth Press, 1972)

Gordon, Lyndall, *Virginia Woolf: A Writer's Life* (Oxford: Oxford University Press, 1984)

Rose, Phyllis, *Woman of Letters: A Life of Virginia Woolf* (London: Routledge, 1978)

Bibliography

Kirkpatrick, B. J., *A Bibliography of Virginia Woolf* (Oxford: Oxford University Press, 1980)

Selected Books and Articles on Virginia Woolf

Abel, Elizabeth, Marianne Hirsch and Elizabeth Langland (eds), *The Voyage In: Fictions of Female Development* (Hanover: University of New England Press, 1983). Includes an essay on *Mrs Dalloway* by Elizabeth Abel

Barrett, Michèle (ed.), *Virginia Woolf: Women and Writing* (London: Women's Press, 1979). Has a substantial introduction, written from a socialist-feminist perspective

Bazin, Nancy Topping, *Virginia Woolf and the Androgynous Vision* (New Brunswick, New Jersey: Rutgers University Press, 1973)

Beer, Gillian, *Arguing With the Past: Essays in Narrative from Woolf to Sidney* (London: Routledge, 1989)

—— 'The Body of the People in Virginia Woolf', in Sue Roe (ed.), *Women Reading Women's Writing* (Brighton: Harvester Press, 1987)

Bowlby, Rachel, *Virginia Woolf: Feminist Destinations* (Oxford: Blackwell, 1988)

—— (ed.), *Virginia Woolf* (London: Longman, 1992). An excellent critical reader.

—— 'Walking, Women and Writing', in Isobel Armstrong (ed.), *New Feminist Discourses* (London: Routledge, 1992)

Caughie, Pamela L., *Virginia Woolf and Postmodernism: Literature in Quest and Question of Itself* (Chicago: University of Illinois Press, 1991)

Defromont, Françoise, *Virginia Woolf: Vers la maison de lumière* (Paris: Editions des femmes, 1985). An extract from this is included in Rachel Bowlby (ed.), *Virginia Woolf*

DeSalvo, Louise, *Virginia Woolf: The Impact of Childhood Sexual Abuse on her Life and Work* (London: Women's Press, 1989)

Ferrer, Daniel, *Virginia Woolf and the Madness of Language*, trans. Geoffrey Bennington and Rachel Bowlby (London: Routledge, 1990)

Flint, Kate, 'Revising *Jacob's Room*: Virginia Woolf, Women and Language', *The Review of English Studies*, XLII, 167 (August 1991), pp. 361–79

Fox, Alice, *Virginia Woolf and the Literature of the English Renaissance* (Oxford: Clarendon Press, 1990)

Fullbrook, Kate, *Free Women: Ethics and Aesthetics in Twentieth-Century Women's Fiction* (Hemel Hempstead: Harvester Wheatsheaf, 1990). Has a stimulating chapter on Woolf

Heilbrun, Carolyn, *Toward a Recognition of Androgyny* (New York: Knopf, 1973)

—— 'Virginia Woolf in Her Fifties', *Twentieth Century Literature*, 27, 1 (Spring 1981)

Hirsch, Marianne, *The Mother/Daughter Plot: Narrative, Psychoanalysis, Feminism* (Bloomington and Indianapolis: Indiana University Press, 1989). Has a section on *To the Lighthouse*

Holtby, Winifred, *Virginia Woolf: A Critical Memoir* (London: Wishart, 1932)

Horner, Avril and Sue Zlosnik, *Landscapes of Desire: Metaphors in Modern Women's Fiction* (Hemel Hempstead: Harvester Wheatsheaf, 1990). Has an illuminating chapter on Woolf

Jacobus, Mary, ' "The Third Stroke": Reading Woolf with Freud', in *Grafts: Feminist Cultural Criticism*, ed. Susan Sheridan (London: Verso, 1988)

Kamuf, Peggy, 'Penelope at Work: Interruptions in *A Room of One's Own*', *Novel*, 16 (Fall 1982)

Knopp, Sherron|E., ' "If I saw you would you kiss me?": Sapphism|and the subversiveness of Virginia Woolf's *Orlando*' in Joseph Bristow (ed.), *Sexual Sameness: Textual Differences in Lesbian and Gay Writing* (London: Routledge, 1992)

Lee, Hermione, *The Novels of Virginia Woolf* (London: Methuen, 1977)

Majumdar, Robin and Allen McLaurin (eds) *Virginia Woolf: The Critical Heritage* (London: Routledge, 1975)

Marcus, Jane, *Virginia Woolf and the Languages of Patriarchy* (Bloomington: Indiana University Press, 1987)

—— (ed.) *New Feminist Essays on Virginia Woolf* (London: Macmillan, 1981)

—— 'Sapphistory: the Woolf and the Well' in *Lesbian Texts and Contexts: Radical Revisions*, ed. Karla Jay and Joanne Glasgow (New York: New York University Press, 1990)

Marder, Herbert, *Feminism and Art: A Study of Virginia Woolf* (Chicago: University of Chicago Press, 1968)

McLaurin, Allen, *Virginia Woolf: The Echoes Enslaved* (Cambridge: Cambridge University Press, 1973)

McNichol, Stella, *Virginia Woolf and the Poetry of Fiction* (London: Routledge, 1990)

Meisel, Perry, *The Absent Father: Virginia Woolf and Walter Pater* (New Haven: Yale University Press, 1980)

Minow-Pinkney, Makiko, *Virginia Woolf and the Problem of the Subject* (Brighton: Harvester Press, 1987)

Naremore, James, *The World Without a Self: Virginia Woolf and the Novel* (New Haven: Yale University Press, 1973)

Rich, Adrienne, 'Motherhood and Daughterhood' in *Of Woman Born: Motherhood as Experience and Institution* (London: Virago, 1977). Includes a discussion of *To the Lighthouse*

Roe, Sue, *Writing and Gender: Virginia Woolf's Writing Practice* (Hemel Hempstead: Harvester Wheatsheaf, 1990)

Showalter, Elaine, *A Literature of Their Own: British Women Writers from Brontë to Lessing* (London: Virago, 1978). Contains an incisive chapter on Woolf

Spivak, Gayatri, 'Unmaking and Making in *To the Lighthouse*' in *In Other Worlds: Essays in Cultural Politics* (London: Methuen, 1987)

Stimpson, Catherine, 'Woolf's Room, Our Project: The Building of Feminist Criticism' , repr. in Bowlby (ed.), *Virginia Woolf*

Trombley, Stephen, *'All that Summer She Was Mad': Virginia Woolf and Her Doctors* (London: Junction Books, 1981)

Ward-Jouve, Nicole, 'A rook called Joseph: Virginia Woolf' in *White Woman Speaks with Forked Tongue: Criticism as Autobiography* (London: Routledge, 1991)

Waugh, Patricia, *Feminine Fictions: Revisiting the Postmodern* (London: Routledge, 1989)

—— *Practising Postmodernism/Reading Modernism* (London: Edward Arnold, 1992)

Both of these contain discussions of *To the Lighthouse*

Woolf, Leonard, *Beginning Again: An Autobiography of the Years 1911–1918* (London: Hogarth Press, 1963)

—— *Downhill All the Way: An Autobiography of the Years 1919–1939* (London: Hogarth Press, 1967)

Index